The Broken Compass

The Broken Compass
How Left and Right
Lost Their Meaning

PETER HITCHENS

continuum

Continuum UK
The Tower Building
11 York Road
London SE1 7NX

Continuum US
80 Maiden Lane
Suite 704
New York, NY 10038

www.continuumbooks.com

First published 2009

British Library Cataloguing-in-Publication Data
A catalogue record for this book is available from the British Library.

ISBN 0187064051

Typeset by Free Range Book Design & Production Ltd
Printed and bound by the MPG Books Group, Bodmin, Cornwall

Contents

Preface

The Lost Frontier

> The creatures outside looked from pig to man, and from man to
> pig, and from pig to man again; but already it was impossible to
> say which was which.
>
> George Orwell, *Animal Farm*

Conventional wisdom is almost always wrong. By the time
it has become conventional, it has ceased to be wisdom and
become cant. Its smug cousin, received opinion, is just as bad.
This is not really opinion at all, but the safe adoption of
whatever is modish and popular. The aim of this book is to
defy these two enemies of thought and reason. They are
powerful in our conformist media, and our conformist media
are powerful in the state, persuading millions to think that the
ideas and beliefs of others are their own, engineering consent
to chosen schemes, denying that consent to ideas they do not
favour.

Conventional Wisdom's biggest single mistake is its
thought-free, obsolete idea of Left and Right. This still relies
on categories and symbols which were dead long ago, and
only kept from decomposing by the refrigeration of the Cold
War: capital versus labour, state control versus free enterprise,
NATO versus the Warsaw Pact, 'democracy versus
Communism', the stuffy censoring establishment versus the

vibrant, unconventional radical fringe. These deserted battle-fields have little to do with the real divisions which now exist between idealist, optimistic 'progressives' and anti-utopian, pessimistic conservatives. Capital and organised labour combine against small business to favour regulation and globalism. Trades Unions long ago abandoned shop-floor struggles, and now mainly act as lobbies for more spending on the public sector where most of their members now work. They also range themselves with multinational corporations in campaigns for globalist and regulatory policies. The NATO alliance symbolises this survival of outward forms, despite the shrivelling away of the conflict that originally created them. The North Atlantic Treaty Organization, bizarrely, continues to exist despite the complete disappearance of the Soviet opponent it was formed to deter.

When Russia recently threatened Georgia, battalions of commentators and politicians in what is still, for lack of a better term, called 'The West' behaved as if this squalid and unimportant territorial squabble between unlovable govern-ments was comparable to the Soviet invasion of Czechoslovakia forty years before. Yet it was wholly different. Russia is no longer an ideological state, externally or inter-nally. It no longer seeks global power, and in some ways is less interested in the minds of its citizens than are 'Western' countries which demand increasing obedience to the formulas of political correctness. In Russia, you may hold what private opinions you like. Just do not challenge the state. In Britain, your private opinions may be reported to the authorities and get you into trouble, even if you believe your actions are part of normal life and you have no wish to challenge the state. This paradox is one of the most alarming facts about the modern world, and is unfortunately too little understood. This is partly because of the growing conventional wisdom that a 'New Cold War' is taking place between tyrannical Russia and free Britain. This is untrue and pernicious. The invented threat abroad is used to justify a stronger state at home.

No doubt the need to preserve its plump apparatus on the outskirts of Brussels partly explains NATO's unresting search for a new enemy, which began in the ruins of Yugoslavia and has now taken it to Afghanistan, about as far from the North Atlantic as it is possible to get. But there is something more. Once a tersely effective and single-minded body, it has become, wordy, utopian and ineffectual – the military arm of the new interventionist idealism. Here as everywhere else in the formerly anti-Marxist 'West', the supposedly beaten Left have become the establishment. The Left and their utopian ideas dominate the civil service, the arts, broadcasting, the academy, the bench of bishops, the courts and the police.

They now censor (and censure) speech and thought, through the formulas of political correctness. They place narrower limits on the speech and writing of others than the Lord Chamberlain ever did on the London stage. At the same time they dispense with any rules that might get in their own way. A liberal will defend to the death your right to agree with her. Disagree with her, and she will call the police.

The defence of 'literary merit' now excuses almost all things which were once taboo, so that *Last Exit to Brooklyn*, once thought grossly disturbing, is tame to the point of dullness by comparison with the general culture. *The Little Red Schoolbook*, once thought too revolting for children, was long ago eclipsed by tax-funded sex education schemes presented to six-year-olds by respectable pedagogues. Some of the 'schoolkids' issue' of *Oz* magazine still has the power to disgust those who exhume it from the archives, especially the obscene version of a Rupert cartoon with its deliberate dirtying of an innocent childhood character. But nobody could be prosecuted now merely for disgusting anyone. The wife of a former prime minister publicly discusses the conception of her youngest child thanks to the lack of 'contraceptive equipment' during a stay at Balmoral. Sexual intercourse is frequently portrayed on mainstream TV channels. In this new mix of licence and censorship, there are new taboos, strange paradoxes and odd reversals. It is a joke to call an airline 'Virgin', but close to an insult to describe an adult as one. The expression 'bastard' can be used freely with one exception. It may not be used as an epithet for a child born out of wedlock. The f-word has become mere punctuation and the failed comedian's standby, while the n-word is (rightly in my view) unsayable by a white person. Those who would once have been the targets of such expressions have special licences to use them, which is strange but defensible. A homosexual can refer to himself as 'queer' and a black person can use the term 'n*****'. But nobody else can. This can be taken to absurd lengths, and is. An employee of the District of Columbia, David Howard, was forced to resign from his post in January 1999 after innocently using the word 'niggardly' – a word which has no racial connotations and certainly had none when he used it. He was eventually rehired by Mayor Anthony Williams, who had at first accepted his resignation. It is perfectly possible to imagine a similar incident in a British town hall or police station.

The sayings and writings of conservative thinkers, and the actions of conservative institutions, are scanned by heresy hunters for evidence of bigotry, and where none is found they are generally accused of it anyway. The charge of 'institutional racism', made against the Metropolitan Police by the Macpherson report into the Stephen Lawrence murder investigation, followed the report's failure to identify any instance of actual racial discrimination. The MP and former army officer Patrick Mercer, a man demonstrably free of racial bigotry, was abruptly fired from the Tory front bench for making a factual statement about the use of racial epithets in the army.

Thanks to this, the defence of dangerous radicalism, the breach of official speech codes, the defiance of cultural norms and moral challenges are left to conservatives and to the old-fashioned type of Christian, who is occasionally questioned by the police for going too far (see the cases of Harry Hammond, Lynette Burrows, Joe and Helen Roberts, and

Stephen Green, described elsewhere by me (esp. in *The Abolition of Liberty*, Atlantic Books, 2004)). Thanks to a curious set of circumstances, it is homosexuality (of all things) that cannot easily be discussed, just as in former days, but for very different reasons. By a cunning switch of logic, opinions on the morality of homosexual acts are no longer treated as opinions, but as 'discrimination' against an officially defined 'minority', an act which is automatically a thought crime. They are also treated as a personal fault or pathology called 'homophobia' (see Chapter 8). Sufferers from this failing are inferior persons not entitled to any consideration in public debate, and automatically in the wrong. Interestingly, the same people are often accused (and convicted without trial) of 'Islamophobia', another unacceptable failing. The paradox, that Islam is (by the same definition) 'homophobic' is often left unexplored.

Leftist and 'progressive' attitudes are now a potent and triumphalist orthodoxy. It is faith, piety, chastity – and attempts to apply Christian belief in public life – which have become outrageous and likely to attract self-righteous derision and even the attention of the law. The Left, which has traditionally been identified with the liberty of speech and thought, or has identified itself with these things, has increasingly become the enforcer of censorship codes.

State ownership of industry is no longer politically important or particularly contentious. Regulation by unaccountable national bodies, and by even more unaccountable supranational and global authorities, has quietly taken its place, with implications that few have yet grasped.

Peace and war, national independence and sovereignty, crime and punishment, religious belief, the marriage bond, the defence of liberty against the bogus claims of fanciful 'security', the limits of personal responsibility and the purpose of education are far more explosive matters. Those demobilised from the disbanded armies of the pre-1989 political world often find themselves in alliances they would never have predicted then, and find awkward now. The real divide between utopian reformer and anti-utopian conservative – which I believe to be the decisive distinction – is now to be found somewhere in the debates about these causes. Conventional thinkers seemed surprised when, in the summer of 2008, the 'Right-wing' Tory MP David Davis and the director of the 'Left-wing' organisation Liberty, Shami Chakrabarti, formed an alliance against the ('Left-wing') Labour government's plan to introduce arbitrary imprisonment. They were further confused when Mr Davis was attacked by the supposedly 'Right-wing' (though by then actually neo-conservative) *Spectator* magazine, and supported by the undoubtedly Left-wing *New Statesman*.

Actually, there was nothing surprising about Mr Davis's behaviour at all to anyone who was not imprisoned by conventional wisdom and received opinion. It was Miss Chakrabarti's position that was more surprising. One of her forerunners in the same post was Patricia Hewitt, herself a classic 1960s Left-winger married to a Left-wing lawyer. Miss Hewitt was for years a senior member of a Cabinet which had supported unceasing attacks on civil liberty. Her fault was not that she vociferously supported these measures. It was that she did not vigorously oppose them. Equally significantly, the 'Left-wing' press had been feeble and mumbling about New Labour's disdain for freedom for most of the period since 1997. Only the principled and determined writings of Henry Porter in *The Observer* saved the Leftist press's reputation during this time. Otherwise, monstrosities such as the Civil Contingencies Act slipped by almost without comment in these quarters.

This is not specially surprising. A little thought will undo the idea that the Left are necessary and reliable supporters of freedom against the state, or that conservatives are automatic supporters of the state against freedom. Proper conservatism, the Burkeian kind, is much attached to liberty and to limited government. But there are other kinds of conservatism that take a different position. Neo-conservatism, a utopian belief developed by disillusioned Trotskyists, is not conservative at all. It is based on a faith in human perfectibility and thinks its holy ends justify its unholy means, as does socialism, even the Fabian variety. People who think themselves benevolent can rarely grasp that others may also think them despotic and are especially bad at recognising that their opponents may have a point. This is why so many of the most repressive regimes in the world, past and present, identify themselves as socialist and attract (or have attracted) some sympathy from the Left – the USSR, the People's Republic of China, the Castros' Cuba, the Democratic Republic of Vietnam.

Meanwhile habitual, tribal, unthinking party-political Conservatism has little connection with the Burkeian ideas it sometimes affects to support. Instead it feigns Churchillian patriotism to cover up for its shame over the loss of empire which it failed to prevent during the first half of the twentieth century. It also finds such bombastic posturing useful to obscure its role in the squalid sale of the country to European Union rule, and in the expedient surrender of this country to the terrorist campaign of the Irish Republican Army. So, to expiate its guilt, it supports all foreign wars, however stupid, generally making false parallels with the war against Hitler (in which its role was also questionable by its own modern standards, especially to start with).

In a constant effort to appear to be what it is really not, it tends to endorse all measures portrayed as guarding this country against the foreign foe, however futile and wrong. At the time of writing, the Conservative Party has supported arbitrary detention up to twenty-eight days, a grave attack on habeas corpus, but is against the extension of this period to forty-two days. It is hard to make out the principle which allows twenty-eight days but forbids forty-two. It also says it is against the introduction of Identity Cards. A few years ago, however, it favoured Identity Cards (so much so that a Tory Home Secretary, Michael Howard, went so far as to produce a Green Paper on the subject). Again, its objections to them do not seem to be principled, but based on grounds of cost and efficiency. It is easy to imagine at least one more zigzag in this course. While the Conservative Party deserves any amount of abuse and mockery for its record on almost everything, this point is important mainly because it illustrates this truth: that unreformed pre-1989 ideas of who is on the 'Left' or 'Right', and what they will do about it, are useless in predicting the behaviour of parties or individuals.

Yet the two main political parties still act and speak as if we were living in the era of the Iron Curtain, of flying pickets, Arthur Scargill and nuclear stalemate with the USSR, when all the 'wasms' were still 'isms'. They realise, of course, that it is not quite so. But most of them cannot work out how or why, because it would be too uncomfortable and disconcerting to do so. So they carry on punching the old buttons and tugging on the old handles, in the hope that the machine will respond as it once did. In 1997, the Tory Party produced a set of unintentionally prophetic posters bearing the slogan 'New Labour – New Danger'. They had no real force of mind behind them, and they failed to stir the voters because nobody could work out precisely what that danger was, and in any case New Labour had the media classes behind it.

Eventually, people inside and outside politics began to see that New Labour was a menace, in some old ways and in some new ones too. It was as committed to high taxation as any previous Fabian socialist government, and determined to create and sustain an enormous clientele of state employees and dependants. It was fanatically egalitarian and regarded the state education system as a tool for creating equality of outcome, not of opportunity. It was anxious to destroy or undermine those parts of the constitution that limited the power and prestige of the executive. It was willing to loosen the Union to the point of dissolution. It was fond of voting systems which empowered party machines, and of postal ballots which were open to abuse. It was righteously hostile to national sovereignty, seeing all patriotism as more or less the same as Slobodan Milošević's Serbian nationalism. It was relentlessly committed to sexual and cultural revolution and to the removal of the privileged position given until now to monogamous, lifelong, heterosexual marriage.

But by the time the Tories had more or less grasped what was really happening, they had also decided that New Labour's policies were not dangerous, but desirable and in fact enviable. In their view, New Labour's policies were not only the route back to office. They were good and acceptable policies which any professional politicians would be wise to adopt. They had very little understanding of the origins of New Labour's radical sexual and family politics, of its hostility to national sovereignty and independence, or of its real Clause Four – its immovable determination to make the state schools into engines of equality. This is expressed through a legal bar on the creation of any new selective state schools, a prohibition which Tory MPs voted for when they supported Labour's 2007 Education Act.

This attitude flows from the fact that (just as most journalists are among the most incurious of beings) few politicians are actually interested in politics. Most Conservative politicians have little grasp of policy or its importance, but are captivated by the prospect of office. It is also because most political Conservatives are rich enough to be immune from the rougher parts of the state school system, and from any regular contact with the officious insolence of local authorities and other government agencies. A large income can and does buy exemption from many of the worst aspects of the New Britain. So most Tories have no real idea of what it is like, and no burning desire to reform it.

They camouflage this lack of political understanding by pretending to be Edwardian country squires and roaring with fake masculinity about how Toryism is a 'disposition, not a dogma'. This may once have been true, when Tories truly were rubicund, weather-beaten, port-soaked countrymen but it is not true of their pasty, suburban successors. Since the arrival of serious, utopian socialism in Britain in the form of Fabianism, the non-socialist parties have had to choose between two responses. Either they must oppose the Fabian dogma in thought and deed, in which case they will need to be dogmatic about what they prefer to it. Or they must accept the arguments of their opponents, while making vague noises of protest to comfort their voters. They have, unsurprisingly, chosen to make the vague noises. It is much easier.

What is the origin of New Labour's dogma? There is Fabianism, still an under-rated force, part of whose cleverness has always been its soothing slowness and gentleness. But now there is also something else, more urgent, more intolerant and more ruthless. It is the Spirit of 1968. Some in New Labour have left trails, which lead back to the days when they were openly committed to the revolutionary change they now secretly espouse. I was present at a conference (organised by 'Index on Censorship') in the summer of 2008 during which Tony McNulty, a Minister of State at the Home Office, announced that he was a former Marxist and so were many of his fellow ministers. He did this in the hope of truckling to any Leftists who happened to be in the audience, and who disapproved of his role in extending arbitrary imprisonment. I do not think he expected his confession to become widely known or reported, and if I had not chanced to have known about this gathering, and so to have written about it, it would have remained largely unknown.

The presence of significant numbers of 1960s revolutionaries in the Parliamentary Labour Party had for years been an open secret at Westminster, though not much known to the public. It was kept very quiet indeed while the Cold War was still in progress. Even after the Cold War was finished, such things were highly sensitive as long as enough people remembered what it had been about.

There are many examples of this. While he was Leader of the Opposition Anthony Blair was so dismayed by truthful revelations that he had been a member of the Campaign for Nuclear Disarmament (CND) that he denied the fact until documentary proof was produced which showed him to be a liar. However, he had by then obtained such total support from the media classes that this shameful behaviour did him no lasting harm. CND, thoroughly misnamed, was not a general pacifist movement. It was a pressure group which sought to make the USSR the only nuclear power in Europe. It had spent its energies campaigning against British and American nuclear weapons, especially during the decisive propaganda battle over medium-range nuclear missiles in the early 1980s. Though it claimed to seek the scrapping of Soviet weapons, it would not have been allowed to do so on the territory of the Warsaw Pact (where official propaganda countered unilateralism with some force). Mr Blair's dalliance with this organisation said more about him, and about his background, than he wished to be known – which is presumably why he tried to lie about it.

His close friend and colleague, Peter Mandelson, was also revealed to have been a member of the Young Communist League, a specifically Communist grouping that a person of his highly political background could not have joined by accident, or without knowing what he was doing. John Reid, who would eventually be Home Secretary and Defence Secretary in the Blair Cabinet, was a former member of the adult Communist Party, which he belonged to at a time when it still supported (and was supported by) the Soviet regime. At least two other members of Mr Blair's first Cabinet are generally believed to have been in – or close to – Trotskyist sects in the 1960s and 1970s, but have never admitted to this in public. Another New Labour figure, also a Cabinet Minister, Charles Clarke, was a former President of the National Union of Students (NUS). The NUS, in the years when he served in this office, was controlled by a close alliance between Labour Left-wingers and open Communists. One of Mr Blair's closest student friends and influences, the Australian Geoff Gallop, was an active member of the International Marxist Group (IMG). The Chancellor of the Exchequer, Alistair Darling, is also said (notably by the Left-wing politicians Tony Benn and George Galloway) to have been a supporter of the IMG, though this has been denied to me personally by 'Whitehall Sources' close to Mr Darling.

These are (more or less) known facts, in almost all cases dragged unwillingly from people who would rather have kept them secret. They are likely to be a small part of the whole story. If individuals do not publicly admit to past membership of Marxist organisations, then it is difficult or impossible for journalists to establish their past links. Membership was seldom publicly declared, and the Communist Party was famous for discouraging influential supporters from joining. Peter Hennessy, in 'The Secret State', records an event in Cambridge in the 1940s where the Communist leader Harry Pollitt advised bright young Communists to stay out of the party and instead to join the establishment. The Trotskyist grouplets of the 1960s and 1970s may not have been so disciplined or thoughtful. But their ambitious student supporters may have been able to make the calculation for themselves. The IMG encouraged its members to use 'cover names' in all written material. I have seen IMG records in which such cover names were used.

One possible source of information has been closed. The Security Service is believed to have destroyed large numbers of files kept during the 1960s on Marxist Left-wingers soon after New Labour came into office in 1997. Mr Mandelson, by then a Minister, publicly urged that this should take place in remarks reported by the *Guardian* on 22 September 1997. On 11 January 1998 the *Sunday Times* carried a story saying that such files were now being destroyed. The Tory MP Julian Lewis drew attention to this odd fact in a brief Commons debate at around this time, and ministers, who attended the debate, noticeably did not take the opportunity to deny it. I sought to obtain details of my own Security Service file, taking my case as far as the Information Tribunal. But my request was denied. I suspect that files on my Trotskyist activities were kept, but have since been destroyed. Almost thirty years afterwards, there was no possible security risk in revealing any surveillance of this kind.

In October 2000, the Glasgow funeral of the former Labour Cabinet Minister, Donald Dewar ended with the playing of the Communist anthem 'The Internationale', which caused many of the congregation, composed largely of 'New Labour' personnel, to hum in tune. Few but ex-Marxists, or current ones, could have had any idea of the significance of this. The *Daily Telegraph*'s account wrongly described the insurrectionary song, the specific property of revolutionary Communists since the Paris Commune of 1871, as 'socialist'. This showed (once again) how little 'professional' political correspondents know about anything. Socialists, and Labour Party loyalists, sing 'The Red Flag'. The 'Internationale', for a time the official anthem of the USSR, has a wholly different significance. I was taught it in English and French in my own revolutionary days and recall it being sung with some brio and force by a Czechoslovak state choir during Mikhail Gorbachev's 1987 visit to Prague. The same disreputable song was part of the Edinburgh funeral of another Scottish Labour Cabinet Minister, Robin Cook. Many members of the Labour establishment, present in force, joined in without hesitation.

What Mr McNulty did not explain in his disclosure was how his thinking had since changed, and what it had changed into. Here I must make an important digression to pre-empt accusations of hypocrisy. Unlike the legions of Labour ex-Marxists, I have never made a secret of my past beliefs and affiliations, and have publicly regretted my past views. Yet in many public debates I have found hostile Labour politicians pointing out to the audience that I am a former Trotskyist, presumably in an attempt to damage me. I contend that my former beliefs are an important key to my current thinking – not least because I understand my current foes far better than if I had never been on their side. I also think my willingness to acknowledge them is an important indicator that I have truly changed my mind. I believe that the secrecy, evasion and embarrassment about their pasts, among Labour politicians, is in a different way a key to understanding their thinking. They do not wish to acknowledge their political pasts because those pasts still have an important influence on their political presents. Here is an example: Mr McNulty's support for detention without trial for six weeks, supposedly justified by national necessity and reasons of state, certainly would not be incompatible with Marxist ways of thinking. Marxists are in charge of many of the most authoritarian states now in existence.

But these days, it is not only revolutionaries who have become relaxed about arbitrary imprisonment and torture. This alliance, in favour of detention without trial, interestingly included former student Trotskyists, now Labour Party grandees, and British fogey Conservatives. These had been propelled by the 'War on Terror' into the embrace of American neo-conservatives, many of whom are also former Trotskyists. From man to pig, and from pig to man. Who would have thought it, in 1968? Or 1988?

The change has placed almost all professional politicians, and many other establishment persons, on one side of the new frontier. This is the reason for the strange softening in the official political borders, which often leads all three major parties to agree on important matters, and makes their MPs increasingly interchangeable. A Parliament which is supposed to be adversarial has become consensual, and serious political debate must usually be held outside Westminster. The organisation 'Intelligence Squared' has proved this in practice with a sparkling series of first-rate contentious debates on many subjects, which have had nothing to do with Westminster alignments. The House of Lords, with its crossbenchers and political pensioners, unconstrained by ambition, has also been a far more interesting chamber than the whipped, obsolescent Commons.

More serious, the demarcation line that is supposed to run down the centre of the Commons chamber now lies between Parliament and the people. Many dangers follow from this. The first is that Parliament, and conventional politics, ceases to interest or engage the mass of the population. This is already happening. The second is that unaccountable extra-Parliamentary forces become dangerously powerful. This is likely to happen soon. The third is that important causes, without any responsible advocates, may fall into the hands of demagogues. The fourth is that Parliament ceases to be adversarial, making our whole society more consensual and less open to debate or dissent. This is visibly taking place. The spectrum of views classified as 'extremist' now covers many opinions which were normal thirty years ago. The spectrum seen as acceptable in normal discourse is extraordinarily narrow.

All these things menace our society with a twin danger of inaction on things that matter, and the growth of forces, with popular backing but without intelligent leadership. This may well destroy liberty and legality. There is still a comfortable layer in our professional and media classes that has yet to feel either of these threats, but this insulation cannot last. Those who live in this relatively safe and prosperous caste need to act, because they have more power and influence than the rest of the population. Inaction is more perilous than action, because of the great length, depth, breadth and height of the issues involved. Our peace and stability as a society are at risk. These blessings are not accidental. They are based on the generally accepted rule of law. Yet that acceptance is shrivelling away. They rely on the ability of an adversarial Parliament to express popular feeling. Yet that Parliament no longer does anything of the kind. It is my belief that our country would be happier and safer if its elite stopped treating important and legitimate political, moral and cultural traditions with contempt.

Part I

The New
Permanent Government
of Britain

1

Guy Fawkes Gets a BlackBerry: A Conspiracy Theory for the Modern Age

This is a curious time for anyone alert to politics and interested in the struggle of ideas. Received opinion and conventional wisdom held for almost ten years that the New Labour government was competent and qualified. They insisted that the Chancellor of the Exchequer, Gordon Brown, was one of the most accomplished holders of his office in modern times. As I write, the very same people and organs of news agree, just as emphatically and just as unanimously, on the hopelessness of Gordon Brown as a person and as a Prime Minister. Opinion polls, the interpretation of election results, cartoons, broadcast comedians and the generally accepted themes of political 'news stories' support and feed on the same theme. Just as there was no significant dissent from the Blairite craze, there is now no significant dissent from its twin, the anti-Brown frenzy. By the summer of 2008, Mr Brown had become the single cause of all ills, from the price of oil to a broken shoelace. A similar unanimity exists about the Tory Party. All political commentators now write or speak as if it is a certainty that the Conservative Party is recovering rapidly and is bound to regain office at the next election. The same facts, analysed more dispassionately, could be used to produce a very different version of events, as I shall explain. For supposedly impartial interpretation of the news has become one of the most powerful tools of modern propaganda.

Michael Dobbs, a former senior official of the Conservative Party, pointed out many years ago in his drawn-from-the-life political thriller *To Play the King*, that opinion polls are a device for influencing public opinion, not a means of measuring it. This is a truth which, once heard and grasped, can never be forgotten or dismissed. But most people have not heard it, and wrongly assume they are being presented with an objective set of facts when they read about an opinion poll in their newspaper. So they are usually bamboozled when the polls, having been subtly angled so as to produce certain required results, are then equally subtly presented so as to obscure several important, unquestionable facts, and to push a suspect, contentious interpretation into the light.

This manipulation is usually not done by the polling organisations, which simply obey their masters and quietly publish the raw facts on their websites, where few will see them. The manipulators are generally the newspapers and the political parties, which pay enormous fees for frequent national surveys. The first contentious step is the framing of the questions, and the order in which they are asked. There are many ways of bending the truth. For example, the interviewee is gently reminded of bad things about the government which he has probably forgotten, by being asked his view of them. Once this softening-up is done, he is then asked for his general opinion of the government or prime minister – which will be significantly worse than if he had been asked the question straight out.

Then there is the treatment of the results. There are two points where this can be influenced. The first is that, since the end of the Cold War, large numbers of voters have refused to say how they will vote, said they would not vote, or said they do not know how they will vote. Another sizeable group say they will vote for parties outside the mainstream. Taken together, this group is now by far the largest in the sample of any telephone poll (YouGov's polls, taken among internet users who are more politically interested, have a significantly lower level of abstentionists). But the newspapers very often leave them out altogether, publishing the result as a three-way fight and failing to mention the respondents who did not fit this picture. If the figures do not show what the newspaper wishes its readers to believe, then they will be buried inside the paper, probably on a left-hand page where fewer people will see them, unadorned by graphics. If the result supports the current view, it will be placed on the front page, accompanied by a dramatic full-colour pie or bar chart. In the early part of 2008, when the Tory poll rating often stayed the same or even fell, the reports would dwell on the fact that the Tory 'lead' had increased, because the Labour rating had fallen. This is a little like saying the pound has risen against the dollar, when in fact all that has happened is that the dollar has fallen while the pound has held its value. But every report, for a reason I will come to, had to give the impression that Labour was failing and the Tories moving towards certain victory. Undoubtedly, this sort of wishful reporting helps to bring about the thing it claims is already happening.

I will doubtless be accused of being a conspiracy theorist for suggesting that the commissioning, selection, timing and media treatment of opinion polls, and the newly merciless portrayal of Mr Brown is in any way co-ordinated or concerted. The accusation is false. I am not a conspiracy theorist in the sense that I search for hidden hands or a single cause behind every event. I do not believe in flying saucers, the grassy knoll theory, the Protocols of the Elders of Zion or anything of the kind. I am sure that the Twin Towers of Manhattan were destroyed by hijacked planes, flown by Islamic fanatics. I do not even believe that the Bilderberg Conference plots the future of Europe. One of my worst failings, as a reporter, is excessive scepticism, which led me to refuse (I feel I can confess it now) to believe the story of the Iraqi 'Supergun' when it was given to me on a plate in a melodramatic phone call. I had perhaps read too many thrillers, and the information sounded to me as if it had been made up by a bad novelist. Sometimes this lack of credulity works in my favour. I can also claim to have smelt a rat when I was invited to be interviewed by an unknown young TV presenter called Ali G, though I had no idea till later just how large and outrageous a rat it was.

But I also know, from direct personal experience, that politicians and political journalists meet incessantly, share similar backgrounds and objectives and – on occasion – plan the co-ordination of policy launches, agree to write articles synchronised with speeches, timed to aid a political objective, and so forth. Those who wish to call such co-ordination 'conspiracy' are free to do so, but by using this silly and misleading term they are blinding themselves to a real process, which takes place often in the modern world. Those who choose to believe that in modern London nobody has confidential discussions to obtain a co-ordinated purpose, in the hope that outsiders are unaware of the collusion, are voluntarily depriving themselves of important knowledge. They are also exposing their naivety about politics and the media. For them, the truth about how much of their daily newspaper has been generated will remain, forever, a mystery. They might, with some justice, be dismissed as 'coincidence theorists', people who believe that apparently co-ordinated events happen fortuitously. It is as likely that crop circles are created by Martian visitors.

The word 'conspiracy' suggests conclaves of sinister armed men in great cloaks and Guy Fawkes hats whispering in taverns by rushlight, with their hands on the hilts of daggers – a scene which seems ridiculously far removed from our world. How can anyone suggest that such things happen in our time? Actually it is this antiquated picture which is ridiculous, and misleading. The confidential co-operation of which I speak is far less picturesque, and a good deal more effective, than anything Guy Fawkes ever did. Those engaged in it wear well-tailored suits, sit in modish, well-lit London restaurants and carry BlackBerries, not daggers. Even so, they do not like others to know what they are up to and are careful to conceal it from the great mass of people who are unaware that it is going on.

Because my arguments are intended to damage the Tories and question their current alleged recovery, I will also be accused of seeking to aid the Labour Party, an allegation which is quite absurd, since that party has been my political enemy for many years and many of its members still blame me personally for helping Neil Kinnock lose the 1992 election in an incident known as 'Jennifer's Ear', which revolved round a misleading Labour election broadcast and a scuffle involving myself and Mr Kinnock. The dislike was still so strong in 1997 that, as I approached the doorway into the press conference launching New Labour's manifesto, two party press officers tried to slam the double doors in my face, absurdly calling out 'It's full up!' like characters from *Alice in Wonderland*. Since then I have been more or less barred from asking questions at any Labour Party press conference. It hardly seems likely that I should now want to help such an organisation, even if I did not disagree with all its policies (as I do) and heartily dislike most of its principal figures (as I do).

And it will no doubt be suggested, by people who know perfectly well that this is not so, that I am trying to defend Gordon Brown. If I do so, it is only a sort of reverse collateral damage (collateral repair? collateral succour?) not intended by me, but sadly inevitable. If I help Mr Brown, I sincerely regret it. It is not Mr Brown I wish to defend. It is the truth, that he is being attacked to ensure political continuity, not because of his actions or his opinions or his abilities. Politically, Mr Brown is virtually indistinguishable from Mr Blair, Mr Cameron or Mr Clegg. That is why the co-ordinated attack on him is almost purely personal, concentrating mainly entirely on his appearance, his demeanour, his character, his lack of glamour, his speaking style, his secretiveness and his obstinacy.

The supposedly political elements of the assault are actually empty. The Tories have no plans to remove the taxes Mr Brown imposed on pension funds. They have never shown any sign of having an alternative scheme for coping with the failure of Northern Rock or the credit collapse in general. The mistake over the abolition of the ten pence tax band was exposed by Labour MPs, not by the Tory Party. The Tory Party only recently discovered an interest in civil liberties after years of eroding them in government. Many of its senior figures are uncomfortable with the current policy and would like to abandon it.

The Conservative Party is in any case just as committed as New Labour to a fiercely egalitarian economic and social policy, combined with very high public spending, and dependent for its success on excessive borrowing. It refuses to distinguish between marriage and other forms of partnership, and regards the discouragement of deliberate single parenthood as discrimination against the single mothers this policy creates each year by the thousand. It entirely and unshakeably supports Britain's membership of the European Union, which means that it cedes 80 per cent of its lawmaking powers, control of the national borders and of trade policy to a foreign power. By implication, it ceases to have any real policies of its own on these topics. Mr Blair, as Prime Minister throughout this policy's implementation, was as responsible for it as Mr Brown is, and as Mr Cameron wishes to be. Yet no comparable attack was made on Mr Blair in office, or since he left office – and Mr Cameron urged his MPs to join in the applause for Mr Blair the day he retired and went off to spend more time with his money.

2

The Power of Lunch:
How Some Events Become News,
and Others Do Not

Anyone who made a serious, coherent political attack on
Gordon Brown and his party would first have to attack
Anthony Blair and then David Cameron and his party as well.
(If they were properly rigorous and honest, they would have to
include John Major and Margaret Thatcher too.) All three men,
and their parties, agree on most major political issues. Politics
is a means of achieving policies, not a soap opera in which
characters who have grown boring or incredible are written
from the script and replaced by new ones, without any real
consequences. The low personal attacks on Gordon Brown, in
many cases by people who never dared to attack him when he
was strong, are despicable because they are cowardly as well
as because they have nothing to do with real politics.

It is time that the important truth about political news
coverage in this country was stated. The electorate are being
manipulated. Maybe they wish to be manipulated, but even
if they do, they should know how it is being done and that it
is being done.

I worked for some years (1984–8) as a political reporter
at Westminster, and learned that there is a strong herd
mentality among these writers and broadcasters which has
little to do with individual political views. In my experience,
political journalists are often fiercely uninterested in political
theory or practice. They generally hold the received
conformist opinions of the 'Centre Left', much as they

9

generally wear suits and ties. It is the done thing. They do not enjoy political arguments about what direction the country should be taking, because they do not much care. They pay little attention to how the country is being governed, or to the implications of legislation passing through Parliament. It astonished me, years after I had left Westminster, when I discovered the nature of several of the Bills that had been passed while I was there. We did not read them. We did not attend the debates about them. We seldom discussed them, either among ourselves or with politicians, being far more interested in faction fights, scandals and 'Who's up? Who's down? Who's in? Who's out?' sorts of gossip.

Political journalists toil in a volatile market, in which certain types of 'news' are highly valued at certain times, but can abruptly lose their value and be displaced by other types, according to the demands and whims of news editors and editors, or of shifting fashions. It is not much less mysterious than the process in the rag trade by which a colour can be on every Paris and Milan catwalk in January and discarded in September. It is probably slightly easier to manipulate. Certain ideas and beliefs, once the political correspondents get hold of them, can determine the way in which every action is portrayed, decide how much prominence an item will receive and the tone of voice in which a subject is dealt with or a minister is addressed by a TV or radio presenter. It simply is not true that the truth will out. If it does not serve the accepted story of the time, it will be ignored, buried or twisted out of shape.

Most news organisations do not really want exclusive or nonconformist reporting. Even exclusive stories must fit the current preoccupations of the pack. The ordinary reader, listener or viewer might think that a reporter should be free to choose what he thinks is important from a politician's speech. But few dare to do so. The correspondents, many of them grown men and women with families, important and respected in their trade, gather in insecure huddles after such orations, to decide what 'the line' shall be.

Worse still, they are often helped towards their decision by public relations men, hired by the politicians to ensure that the correct message is understood as they wish it to be understood and in no other way. The evaluation and rating of major speeches (which is usually strangely unanimous) can be altered if it does not fit in with what the consensus of editors has agreed is the 'correct' interpretation. Writers who have given unflattering accounts of platform performances by rising politicians have been known to receive anxious phone calls from their superiors – better informed about which way the wind is blowing – forcefully urging them to change their opinions. They have usually obeyed. Anthony Blair was turned into a popular craze, a process aided by the mysterious intangible qualities from which stardom can be made. It is not so easy to do this for David Cameron, who – being more intelligent and informed than Mr Blair – lacks the vacuous, narcissistic Princess-Diana-like sparkle and glitter which the leader of New Labour possessed.

Mr Cameron has so far succeeded by simultaneously obtaining exaggerated praise for himself, and benefiting from exaggerated abuse of his most pressing opponent. His supposedly brilliant speech at the Tory conference of 2006 would not now stand much analysis or cold-eyed viewing. Hardly anyone can recall a word he said, just as few who praise the novels of Salman Rushdie can say how they end, and just as few who revere the poet Ted Hughes can quote a memorable line from his verse. Bandwagon popularity does not require substance.

The point was that his rival, David Davis, had allegedly made a speech that was so very much worse. Was it? There can be no independent tribunal on such things. Neither speech was spectacularly good or bad, though Mr Davis's was certainly more pedestrian. I was standing in the hall during both of them, close to the platform. What surprised me was the unanimous frenzy of contempt directed at Mr Davis by my fellow-journalists, and the equally single-minded Niagara of praise for Mr Cameron. Some weeks later, by most objective

opinion, Mr Davis did markedly better than Mr Cameron in
a televised debate in which knowledge and experience counted,
but this was too late to alter the assessment. Mr Cameron was
already anointed. The coronation had already been arranged.
The media mind was made up, and their decision was final. The
Tory Party and its MPs had the sense to see who the most
powerful electorate in the country had chosen, and to endorse
their choice. Only a personal scandal – and even then, only a
really potent scandal – could have altered the outcome. Mr
Cameron's problems over drug use, combined with his support
for weaker drug laws, which would have destroyed his
candidacy only five years before, never received the concentrated, relentless treatment reserved for those politicians whom
the media gods wish to destroy. But an interview with Mr
Davis's wife, in which she was unwisely frank over some
harmless details of their home life, continued to hurt Mr Davis
for weeks afterwards, like poison in the bloodstream.

There was a remarkable consensus among those reporting
the Blackpool speeches, some of whom were quick to turn to
their neighbours after Mr Cameron's oration and say it was
brilliant, and to turn to their other neighbours after Mr Davis's
contribution and to sigh about its awfulness. Crucially, the main
political correspondents of the TV stations did something
similar, using their immense power to make decisive judgements
whose effect they must have been able to guess. Technically,
such judgements are not breaches of impartiality. But they are
a specially clear example of the way in which apparently
dispassionate analysis can influence contentious decisions.

I must here mention that I had a bias of my own, since I had
always got on well with David Davis, and had known him for
some time, whereas at the time of the speech I had not even met
David Cameron (I have since, and have not changed my view
as a result). He would certainly not have considered me a
potential ally. I had written a critical column about Mr
Cameron's support for the relaxation of the cannabis laws, his
only political action of any significance since he had entered
Parliament. I recall mildly disagreeing with one of Mr

Cameron's enthusiasts in the Blackpool Winter Gardens, a journalist with whom I had until then been on reasonably good terms. My dissent was met with something close to fury that I was not one of the brotherhood. (Since then I have regularly been targeted for much worse abuse by another prominent media supporter of Mr Cameron, who growls and rumbles at me whenever we meet.)

If this response, 'Davis atrocious, Cameron wonderful', was not co-ordinated or 'briefed' in any way, then either there must have been the most tremendous series of coincidences or there must have been something in the Blackpool water that day. An enormously wide variety of reporters and sketch-writers unanimously supported it. Was it really possible that so many highly different people, of many backgrounds, tastes and varying educations, working for this country's astonishing breadth of media outlets, could all have spontaneously thought the same thing? There is a simpler explanation. The techniques, long pioneered by New Labour and well known to attenders of conferences, were not exactly secret – the 'friends' warned and positioned in advance to clap enthusiastically and encourage a standing ovation, the friendly journalists primed to form and harden the opinions of others. Could such things have been going on? We will have to wait for the memoirs before we know. But, given Mr Cameron's background in professional public relations and his membership of the London media class, I think it unwise to rule out the use of these or similar methods.

Perhaps the explanation lies in mass psychology. Perhaps it lies in the lunching habits of Fleet Street (see below). Perhaps it is simply driven by career pressures. Far from welcoming individualistic, enterprising journalism, most media executives on daily papers and in TV organisations are unsettled by it. It makes them feel nervous and exposed. If their own outlet is leading with its own story, and every other outlet is leading with a conformist story, they will feel much more comfortable once they have switched their lead to follow the flock. This can lead to ridiculous behaviour In the long-ago days of direct rivalry between the *Daily Express* and the *Daily Mail*, in the early 1970s, the two papers would sometimes exchange front-page lead stories during the evening, as the night editors of both felt such a strong desire to follow where the other had led. This of course involved displacing the stories their own men had found and written. I recall, in the early 1980s, straining in vain for weeks to get a certain story into the *Daily Express*, for which I then worked – until in despair I gave it to a friend working for the *Sun*, which led its first edition with it. The night news desk were too embarrassed to ask me to follow it up, though they must have yearned to do so.

And there is a process, described by Peter Oborne with great candour, by which only certain types of stories can win prominence (and so advance the careers of their authors) at certain times and seasons. Oborne wrote in the *Spectator* of 21 June 2003:

> I was unable to cope when I joined the parliamentary lobby as a reporter for the *London Evening Standard* more than ten years ago. I faced two problems, both of them disastrous. The first was that I did not know how to recognise a political story. A grand set-piece – the sacking of a minister, or the fall of a government – was obvious enough to anyone. But the kind of event that fills the newspapers on a daily basis appeared to me arbitrary, governed by laws that I could not fathom. The second problem was even worse. Once a story had been drawn to my attention, I did not know how to write it.
>
> It was a bad time. I acquired a haunted look, lost more than a stone in weight and daily expected to be dismissed by the editor of the *Evening Standard*, to me at least a remote and ferocious figure. Late one evening I humbly approached a senior member of the lobby for advice. 'You have to bear one thing in mind, lad,' the old-timer told me. 'The reader does not want to look at the story at all. He is heading straight to the theatre listings or the sports pages. Your job is to arrest his attention before he gets there.

'A political story,' he explained, 'is essentially composed of two elements. Something happens – a speech, a piece of economic news, a throwaway remark by a Cabinet minister, a resignation. But these events, by themselves, have no meaning. They have to be connected with a wider pattern.

'Thus an article that starts off: "The rate of inflation rose by x per cent last night," while accurate so far as it goes, is unlikely to hold the reader's attention for long. A story that begins "The government was plunged into economic crisis last night as the rate of inflation leapt by a shock x per cent" has a greater chance of success.'

From that moment my fortunes started to improve. This was the early 1990s, and John Major's government was in the process of establishing its reputation for sleaze, incompetence and indiscipline. Soon a structure was in place which transformed minor and often innocent transgressions by government ministers into blazing front-page stories. Coveted space on the front page could be obtained by the simple expedient of beginning with the phrase 'John Major faced a fresh sleaze crisis last night as ...'.

The same magic was capable of converting remarks by obscure Tory backbenchers into a nutritious page-one splash, usually kicking off with something like: 'The Tory party broke wide open over Europe last night as ...'. These admittedly mechanical routines went on bearing fruit till the government of John Major was finally put out of its misery in the 1997 general election.

The by no means negligible achievement by the Downing Street director of communications, Alastair Campbell, has been to prevent the same syndrome emerging under New Labour. Tony Blair's government is every bit as 'sleazy' and incompetent as John Major's – in truth, very much more so.

Campbell has used his art to ensure that the numerous Labour corruption stories have been treated as discrete events, not part of a vicious, self-fulfilling pattern. The methods used – manipulation of the news agenda, creation of a claque of friendly journalists, the use of access as a means of control, above all an unspoken deal with News International – are neither heart-warming nor attractive. But they have been undeniably effective. Bad stories about New Labour have found it hard to get off the ground because Fleet Street has been unable or unwilling to place them in a broader context.

When Oborne wrote this, he believed – prematurely, as it happened – that Labour's media luck was about to run out. In fact, Mr Blair's apparatus and the Blair claque operated pretty much to the end of his period as Prime Minister. What puzzled (and, I suspect infuriated) many of those involved is that Gordon Brown's initial few months did not result in an immediate collapse, as many of them had hoped and some had predicted. On the contrary, many commentators were relieved to be rid of the blithe fraudulence of his predecessor. The Cameron supporter and *Times* columnist Matthew Parris, now one of Mr Brown's most merciless persecutors, wrote at the time that it was quite extraordinary how nobody missed Anthony Blair at all. On 11 August he wrote in *The Times* of the 'national relief' that had greeted Mr Brown and said 'Now that he has gone, the nation is not pining for its previous Prime Minister, as most of us predicted. Britain does not seem to be missing him at all.' He would have found it hard to stand by that article six months later, given the implication of his persistent theme in more recent articles, that Mr Brown lacks Mr Blair's personal and dramatic skills.

The flock did not turn on Mr Brown until he allowed his supporters to speculate that he might call a snap election, and then did not call it. From that moment every Brown failing has been, as Oborne terms it 'part of a vicious, self-fulfilling pattern'. It is interesting to note that this transformation happened when the media felt cheated of something they greatly wanted *for themselves*, and so were genuinely inflamed with real wrath on their own behalves. They were deprived of an election they had begun to hope for – an election which, for political journalists, is an occasion of joy and excitement comparable, say, to the Cheltenham Festival for race-goers, or the World Cup for football enthusiasts. It is hard not to suspect that personal disappointment played a part in the rage that followed. A Left-wing commentator, David Aaronovitch (*The Times*, 29 April 2008) expressed bafflement at the sudden, total turn.

> You get a better write-up in *The Guardian* if you are Fidel Castro or the leader of Hamas than if you're the Labour Prime Minister. Despite them rooting for Mr Brown when the hated Blair was in power, they now seem to concur that GB ought to be someone else, someone able to emote over the plight of mortgage-holders, someone as decisive as Tony Blair was over, say, Iraq. They adored Mr Brown for being Mr Notblair ('look, no grandstanding') in the summer, but the moment that things got rough, they plunged into the water and made for their nests on Purity Island.

But in the same article, he hinted at a reason for the transformation.

> Mr Brown, damaged by his own treatment of his predecessor, has made several tactical mistakes and one strategic error. He didn't realise how quickly one dominant narrative can be replaced by another, and he failed to hold the election that could have saved him. The result has been that, for six months, no one has asked the Government anything but the most hostile questions, and no one has asked David Cameron any difficult ones. The next election is being won and lost by default.
>
> The question that centre-left progressives like me will have to answer is whether we're bothered. Tony Blair's mission, unexplained even to himself perhaps, was to make it not matter whether the Tories came back, as they

would be hemmed in by Blairism just as Labour was by Thatcherism.

This belief is interestingly echoed by the *Independent* commentator Steve Richards (see below, p. 32) but Mr Richards is quite sure that Mr Blair and his colleagues fully understood this part of their project, and Mr Blair spoke words in 2001 (see below, p. 32) which confirm this was so. Mr Aaronovitch (a former Communist) says he is not as complacent as the 'Guardianistas' about the safety of the Blair project in Tory hands. But, unsupported by facts or logic, this is merely a quiver of vestigial tribal feeling.

The other important thing which the outsider must grasp is that British journalism is full of discreet collusion between writers and politicians, which is known as 'lunch' or (when more weighty issues are involved) takes the form of secretive dining clubs in which political figures urge journalists to float certain ideas on their behalf, in a co-ordinated fashion. I will not go into details about such clubs, beyond stating the fact that they undoubtedly exist, because their activities are ruled by a deadly *Omertà* only slightly less strict than that of the Cosa Nostra.

As for the lunches, I can freely say that I have eaten many of them, and the convention is that in return for costly food and drink in an over-priced London restaurant, the minister or shadow minister provides gossip and a leak, which serve the interest of the politician, and which are then published in concert by the two or three journalists present (only the very senior correspondents lunch important ministers alone). It must not be blatantly linked to the source. He must certainly not be named, and 'footprints' which might give insiders a clue to the source must be avoided. Non-members of the Parliamentary lobby are largely excluded from this major cottage industry, which is in constant busy action and must turn over many thousands of pounds a week.

I was once lunching with a Labour MP in a rather political Covent Garden restaurant and was amused when the former

Chancellor, Kenneth Clarke, sat down at the next table with two lobby journalists. He recognised me (I am a critic of Mr Clarke's positions on the European Union and a number of other things. I once publicly offered him a Labour Party membership form). After much urgent whispering and several worried glances across the room, the journalists asked the head waiter to move them to a table on the far side of the room. The following day a story about policy on the EU, unhelpful to the then leader of the Tory Party, and helpful to Mr Clarke, appeared in two major newspapers. It would be wrong to use the word 'conspiracy' to describe this outcome (for reasons explained above). But it would be even more wrong to use the word 'coincidence'. It undoubtedly involves co-ordinated actions confidentially agreed by interested parties, without the knowledge of many of those who will be affected by the result. It is more polite to call it lunch.

These lunches are not as partisan as newspaper readers might expect. Journalists of the Left have good lunching and telephone relations with politicians who are at least nominally on the Right, though in my experience things do not work quite so smoothly when conservative reporters have to deal with Left-wing politicians. Not that there are many conservative reporters, in the nature of things, given that political journalists are generally recruited from among post-1968 university graduates. The Left-wing politicians also really are on the Left, whereas most of the officially Right-wing ones are not really on the Right.

What matters is how useful the journalist can be to the politician. Often, an apparently hostile medium is more useful than an apparently friendly one. Here is an example. I can recall, at one of Britain's many literary festivals, sharing the supper table with two prominent BBC presenters who spent the entire evening urgently and sympathetically discussing Michael Howard's impending takeover of the Tory Party from Iain Duncan Smith. Only three days before, Mr Howard had flatly and unequivocally denied to a group of conservative reporters (including me) that he had any interest in seeking the Tory crown. The two BBC presenters clearly had better information, and it was easy to work out how they had come by it and why. The BBC understood that Mr Howard's takeover of the Tory Party was an event of great significance for British politics as a whole, and one they approved of. Mr Howard would have had reason to expect – and be glad of – BBC support and encouragement for his action. Conservative journalists and papers, on the other hand, would just have to take what they were given. Where else could they go?

The BBC's part in the liberal takeover of the Tories is mostly invisible, though sometimes it bursts into the open in extraordinary actions by the Corporation. The current relations between the BBC and the Tory Party are secretive and increasingly important. They need to be. The BBC helped bring about the defeat of the Tories in 1997, not least by making an issue out of the number of Tory candidates who opposed deeper integration into the EU, and relentlessly presenting this rather predictable and unsurprising fact as a damaging split. Such reporting falls way beyond its remit as an impartial broadcaster, or would do, if it had such a remit. However, the BBC does not think it should be impartial over several issues – the EU being one of them.

It is also skilled at obeying the strict formal rules of balance and equal time, while using subtlety to express its real feelings. In the final years of the Major government, BBC interviewers were far more aggressive towards Tory spokesmen than towards Labour ones. Where they were critical of Labour ministers after 1997, the questions were generally formulated from a position some way to the left of Labour's, based on the assumption that New Labour was in some way betraying its Left-wing roots. On one occasion, during Labour's first major assault on the hereditary peers in the House of Lords, the *Newsnight* interviewer Jeremy Paxman was questioning the then Tory leader William Hague. Mr Hague was trying to resist the changes but had been undermined by his own leader in the Lords, whom he had reasonably sacked as a result. Mr

Paxman became dissatisfied with Mr Hague's responses to his questions and invited a Labour spokesman, also present in the studio, to take over the questioning. The idea that Mr Hague might have any sort of case was never even considered. There was no scandal over this.

During the early years of the Blair government, controversies between Labour and the Tories were generally presented by means of the technique known as the 'sandwich'. Formal impartiality was achieved by giving time to a Tory and a Labour spokesman (government first, opposition second). But the reporter would then complete the item by giving a further response (and the decisive last word) to unnamed government sources (thus, 'government-opposition-government', hence 'sandwich'). Tones of voice, facial expressions, timing and general selection all favoured the Labour government, as did the fact – confirmed in a dangerous book by the former BBC staffer Robin Aitken – that political conservatives are largely missing from the BBC's staff.

In Mr Aitken's book *Can We Trust the BBC?* (Continuum, London, 2008) he summarises the set of positions which together shape the BBC's involuntary, largely unconscious bias. This bias, as will be clear, was not a direct and blatant party-political one. It is a world-view, seen by those who hold it as the only morally acceptable one. This made it physically unable to give fair treatment to the pre-Cameron Conservative party. Mr Aitken explained (pp. 12–13), 'The BBC is passionately against racism, in favour of "human rights", supportive of internationalism, suspicious of traditional British national identity and consequently strongly pro-EU; it is feminist, secular and allergic to established authority, whether in the form of the Crown, the courts, the police or the churches.' In my view, Mr Aitken should have placed the word 'racist' in inverted commas in this description. Who, after all, is not biased against racial bigotry? But this interesting word, while intended to suggest racial bigotry and certainly encompassing many people who are racial bigots, has a far wider application (see chapter 8). Unlike the older usage, 'racialist', it is also used to refer to those whose concerns are purely cultural, and who have no racial prejudice. For instance, most BBC staff would readily apply it to an opponent of mass immigration from Eastern Europe, where 'race', as normally understood, is not involved, and colour certainly is not.

After the election of Mr Cameron as Tory leader, this changed in a startling fashion. BBC radio bulletins began to treat Mr Cameron with respect. Tory political initiatives were reported as news items in their own right. The party was referred to as 'The Conservatives' rather than 'The Tories'. Its front-bench spokesmen were referred to as 'Shadow Chancellor' or 'Shadow Foreign Secretary'. In the Blair years they had often been deprived of this dignity and treated as more or less equal to the far smaller Liberal Democrats.

My *Mail on Sunday* colleague Miles Goslett made a number of Freedom of Information requests early in 2008 to discover if the BBC had met Mr Cameron, and to see if any specific instructions had been issued on the treatment of the 'modernised' Tory Party. The Corporation reluctantly and slowly disgorged the fact that the BBC Director General, Mark Thompson, had met Mr Cameron for private talks. Mr Thompson, and his chief political commissar Caroline Thomson (wife of the New Labour figure Roger Liddle and daughter of the late Labour MP and Liberal Democrat peer Lord Thomson of Monifieth) travelled to Westminster on 28 February 2008 to pay court to the Tory leader. At the time of writing, Mr Goslett's efforts to discover the contents and extent of this conversation have so far failed. Other meetings, between BBC officials and the relevant Shadow Cabinet member, have also taken place at which standard policy questions could have been addressed. It seems reasonable to assume that Mr Thompson, accompanied by Ms Thomson, would have met Mr Cameron himself only to discuss macro-politics.

The Corporation cited two separate clauses of the Freedom of Information Act to justify its flat refusal to say what had been discussed at this event. One of these clauses, a general escape, says items touching on the BBC's journalism are not covered by the Act. The other, more rarely invoked, excuses silence with the claim that politicians and the Corporation have the right to have confidential conversations. The Corporation also refused to answer a question inquiring into any memos or instructions on the coverage of the party. Both queries, at the time of writing, are still being considered by the Information Commissioner.

3

'Time For a Change':
Why People Who Have No Opinions
Want the Tories to Win

I long ago abandoned the world of full-time political reporting without regret and went off into the outside world. Even so, I have great respect for the few individuals in political journalism, including several of my colleagues at the *Mail on Sunday*, who do not follow the bleating flock. But I am highly suspicious of its role in influencing the leadership choices of political parties. And I am still more suspicious of its current attempt to create a Tory revival when there ought not to be one. One aim of this book is to make a modest effort to frustrate this exercise, whose motives are for the most part shockingly non-political, but need to be understood by any intelligent newspaper reader, viewer or listener.

Political journalists advance their careers by becoming the conduits of lunch-time leaks, as explained in chapter 2. They begin as lowly 'number-threes', the subalterns of the trade. They may even need to slave before the mast as 'number fours'. Political staffs have actually expanded as other departments have dwindled and vanished. Industrial and labour reporters are all but extinct. Trial reporting is a vestige of what it used to be. So, paradoxically, is the old-fashioned type of crime reporting. Even the most exalted organs have reduced their foreign staffs, and diminished the space they provide for overseas reports. Political stories have filled much of the gap, especially in the BBC, in middle market and unpopular papers. This is only untrue at the bottom of the market. The

Red Top papers have nearly abandoned serious coverage of anything (which several of them used to try manfully to provide) and for them politics is, most of the time, a branch of the celebrity industry.

In a country with a steadily diminishing supply of real power, the coverage of politics has increased when it really should have declined. But that is largely because it is not about power and its exercise, but about the soap opera drama of personality, rivalry and chicanery. It is also because many (not all) editors tend to like to have contact with ministers, and to enjoy the flattering attention, and the feeling of closeness to power, which Downing Street can give them. The political soap opera also helps to fill the pages which would once have been filled by criminal trials (seldom reported unless exceptional nowadays) or by foreign despatches. Britain has also become so strange in the past few years that many events which would have once demanded a page to themselves are now seen as normal, crimes especially having been devalued so that murders that would once have featured in national newspapers are now buried inside regional evenings.

If apprentice political journalists choose their contacts wisely, feed them generously and court them carefully and long, they will eventually become full members of the Westminster Clubhouse. Then they can impress their editors with an uninterrupted series of medium-calibre stories, especially useful on Monday mornings or during the long summer news famine, when pages must be filled with something, even if it is a crisis in the Liberal Democrats – such things really have been front-page lead stories in *The Times* in the dog days of August. In this way they slowly advance to the position of 'number two'. From there they can hope to grasp the prize of their careers – flag rank, the political editorship, which confers high status in their offices and among politicians, and which, in many organisations, can lead on to executive posts and even editorships, where the pay is at last something like what the public imagines it to be.

Political editors become identified with, and close to, the government in office. The senior reporters and senior ministers will have grown up with each other, and grappled their way up the greasy poles of their similar trades together. These days they may well be around the same age (older politicians having been largely got rid of during the Blair age). They may well have attended the same universities. In the case of New Labour, many journalists played a large and active part in helping to create the New Labour brand, and then in putting Mr Blair and his colleagues in office. Some of these were rapidly rewarded by being given posts under the Blair government, others served that government less directly. In the distant days of Margaret Thatcher and John Major, they were mostly number twos and threes, excluded from the ageing Tory inner circle and compelled to make friends with Labour MPs in the hope that they might one day be in the Cabinet. Alastair Campbell chose (and fed with carefully designed stories) a good number of them – in the hope (not always unjustified) that they would be his allies afterwards, accepting and placing stories helpful to Mr Campbell and damaging to his opponents.

Now their younger would-be successors have spent many years, and thousands of pounds, lunching obscure young Tory MPs in the hope that they will one day be on easy telephone terms with Conservative Cabinet Ministers. In some cases, they also no doubt hope for government jobs. They have waited, in their view, quite long enough. Lunch has been served over and over again. Now they wish to present the bill. But they cannot, unless their contacts actually become the government – and it was clear by 2007 that this was by no means certain and that the famous political pendulum might need to be pushed a little before it would swing.

This was no small thing for a reporter who had spent much of his life investing in a change which might not happen. Another seven years of New Labour would have meant another seven years of being on the outside. Worse, it could have meant that all those meals had been entirely in vain, those premature double chins and 36-inch waists acquired for nothing. The Tories, likewise, grew impatient. They had enjoyed the food, but they now wanted another sort of meat. They wanted ministerial offices, chauffeured cars, respectful civil servants, red boxes, large salaries, the many joys and consolations of office, even if they did not get any power. They longed to have their own tame lobby flock, to whom they could leak stories which suited their careers and their ends. Meanwhile, the existing political editors grew weary of the repetitive round and sought promotion to exalted, less hectic posts as columnists or executives. Their ministerial contacts began to think of memoir-writing, speech-making or well-rewarded directorships and consultancies. No wonder there was such a desire for a change of government among the political and media classes by the autumn of 2007. But it had nothing whatever to do with the needs of the country, which are seldom discussed at this insulated and comfortable level.

So the reader or viewer is not imagining it when he suspects that there is a significant change of tone in what he reads, hears and sees. After ten years in which the Tory Party was treated as a laughable outcast, it is particularly startling to see how things have altered. Are Tory spokesmen and ideas being treated with more respect? Do interviewers keep trying to seek out division and dissent in New Labour, when before they never did? Are the questions selected for programmes such as *Question Time* somehow more dangerous to the government than they were? Are the stories chosen to lead the front pages more often matters of dismay and alarm? Are the screen captions on the rolling news channels obsessively concerned with subjects such as 'Brown's Woes – latest'? Are the photographs of the Prime Minister more often taken from unflattering angles and at awkward moments? Are reporters on Parliamentary debates more likely to editorialise critically about ministers' performances? Yes, they are. Is impartial political 'analysis' filled with discussion about the troubles of Labour and the recovery of the Tory Party? Are the cartoonists of the Left-wing papers more than usually savage towards Mr Brown? In all cases, the answer is 'Yes.' Do those who are doing this even realise what they are doing? In many cases, they probably do not. Yet from their private conversation it is clear that they have swallowed the view that it is now the turn of David Cameron's Tories to win an election.

The facts revealed by a careful reading of the opinion polls and of recent actual elections are not so straightforward. The major polls routinely discard the answers of between 33 per cent and 37 per cent of respondents, who in one way or another refuse to reveal their allegiance. This is a larger portion of the electorate than that supported by any party, none of which has recently scored much above 28 per cent of the voting roll. These facts are quite properly revealed in the detailed workings on the websites of the polling organisations. But they are buried, or actually suppressed, in the newspapers which paid for the surveys and which publish them. In two recent sets of local elections, lazy and self-servingly credulous journalists have readily accepted claims of a major Tory advance. But detailed study of these contests, where possible, shows that the advance is minor, and on such a low poll that it is unreliable as a guide. The claim that the Tories scored 44 per cent of the vote in the May 2008 local elections is based not on a proper count (which would be very difficult and time-consuming) but on a small sample. In any case 44 per cent of 36 per cent (the average turnout) is not a particularly impressive figure.

By-election results are a poor guide to general elections, since voters are quite intelligent enough to realise that their decisions will not change the government, and so feel free to break with normal allegiances. This used to be quite well known to political reporters, who covered these strange events routinely. But a recent drop in the average age of MPs has meant a lower death rate and a sharp decline in the frequency of by-elections, so this lesson seems to have been forgotten. The extrapolations made after the Crewe and

Nantwich poll of May 2008 were, perhaps as a result, quite absurd. Mrs Thatcher sustained several by-election defeats just as striking, but they had no bearing on the general elections which followed. Such elections allow party machines to concentrate their entire force on one small area, an effort normally quite impossible, so distorting the outcome. They also sometimes come under the national microscope, in ways which influence voters strongly. Newspapers would never normally commission a full-scale opinion poll, which costs around £10,000, for a single constituency. When people become aware that their individual vote may affect the result, which they do because of such polls, they behave quite differently.

In Bromley South, the first test of David Cameron's leadership, there was no such spotlight, and the Tory candidate did very badly. Yet there was no extrapolation that the Cameron project was doomed. The same was true in Dunfermline. In South Ealing, national disclosures that the Tory candidate had been photographed with Mr Blair shortly before, ensured that he failed dismally. Again, few extrapolated from this that Mr Cameron was finished. Crewe and Nantwich arrived at a moment when many forces were poised to affect its result, and they duly did. Something similar, though more specifically Scottish, happened in Glasgow East – where the anti-Labour (but not specifically pro-Tory) character of the mood change produced a feeble Tory vote and a Scottish Nationalist victory. The main reason for the collapse of these safe Labour majorities was not a public swing to another political position – the policies of the Tories are almost identical to those of Labour in England, and the SNP stands marginally to the left of Labour in Scotland. It was that the political media class were at last ready for a new government and had assiduously prepared the conditions for it.

But they are ready for this to happen for the oddest reason. They desire a different government, not because it will bring about change, but because it will not.

They base their arguments on completely unpolitical matters such as 'competence' or 'sleaze', or the personality of the head of government. They pretend that the Labour Party's fund-raising methods are more suspect than those of the Tories, when ten years ago these same people were pretending the precise opposite. They believe that one group of professional politicians will somehow be more competent than another – an odd claim, given that, if these people are competent at all in governing the country, it is because they have had some experience of doing so, which for most of them is the only knowledge of government or management they have had in their whole lives. How then can it be beneficial to replace them with another group of amateurs without any experience at all?

4

Fear of Finding Something Worse:
Why the Left Want to
Save the Tories

Anyone who looks carefully at these matters discovers a truth that is much more interesting and far more significant than the silly personal attacks which pass for political debate in the House of Commons. A major constitutional shift has taken place in one of the great organs of the state. The Conservative Party is being allowed another chance at office only because it is pledged to continue to govern as Anthony Blair and Gordon Brown have governed. Labour, which for decades sought to attain irreversibility of its reforms by securing two successive election victories with full working majorities, has now reached the most significant moment in its entire history, the complete acceptance of its programme by the Conservatives. This has been tacitly admitted in the Tories' long-term failure to oppose Labour's large increases in public spending and taxation, their unwillingness to oppose Labour's constitutional changes, their acceptance of the comprehensive schooling system, and their surrender to Labour's programme of sexual and cultural revolution. Both parties have been in agreement for twenty years on support for British membership of the European Union, and – despite some posturing – the Tory position on this remains fundamentally the same as the government's.

This has never happened before on such a scale. The capitulation of the official Opposition to the programme of the government is far deeper and wider than the only other such surrender of this kind in British political history, the Tory decision in 1950 to leave Labour's 1945 nationalisations and welfare measures largely untouched. Even more significant, David Cameron's acceptance of the Blair legacy is an implicit apology for Margaret Thatcher's partly successful attempt to reverse the 1945 revolution. Mr Blair specifically demanded such a change, during the 2005 election, as the price for allowing the Tory Party back into the magic circle of office. He said in Wellingborough on 5 June 2001, just before the campaign ended:

> At this election we ask the British people to speak out and say the public services are Britain's priority, to say clearly and unequivocally that no party should ever again attempt to lead this country by proposing to cut Britain's schools, Britain's hospitals and Britain's public services. Never again a return to the agenda of the eighties.

This was extraordinarily significant, which is probably why it was entirely ignored by every political journalist in the country, since most political journalists are profoundly bored by pure politics. Its significance was confirmed some time later, when Steve Richards, one of those well-connected commentators who move so seamlessly between the BBC and the Left-wing press, had this arresting piece of information for the readers of the *Independent on Sunday* (7 October 2001):

> At the last [May 2001] election Tony Blair and his entourage were often in an exasperated fury. The media and the voters were stubbornly indifferent to what they considered to be a defining moment. 'You don't get it,' they would occasionally scream, 'the election is a historic referendum on a right-wing Conservative party. If we win a second landslide we would kill off right-wing Conservatism for good.'

Mr Blair was following a long tradition of his party, which has since the 1930s been trying to devise ways of making its actions irreversible, so that it could lose office for a time and still return to continue its transforming project. Edmund Dell, in his superb history of the Labour Party (*A Strange, Eventful History*, HarperCollins, London, 2000), dwelt on Labour's deep yearning for a full second term to make its changes irreversible. Capital taxes, he pointed out, are slow-acting and will not work their egalitarian purpose unless they are kept up for decades. Aneurin Bevan reckoned in May 1945 that a full twenty-five years in office would be needed to achieve socialism (speech to the Labour Party Conference, Blackpool, 21 May 1945). His words are interesting not only because nobody would now use them but because he was without doubt speaking the truth:

> We enter this campaign not merely to get rid of the Tory majority – that will not be enough for our task. It will not be sufficient to get a parliamentary majority. We want the complete political extinction of the Tory Party and 25 years of Labour government. We cannot do in five years what requires to be done.

In 1932, the Labour intellectual Harold Laski had argued that 'for the preservation of parliamentary democracy', a future Labour government should ask for guarantees from the Conservative Party that it would not repeal Labour legislation if it returned to office (article in *The New Statesman*, 10 September 1932). As Dell says: 'This was not, and could not be, the position of the Labour Party. Yet it left open the question how a Labour government, using constitutional means, could keep itself in power for the long period required actually to achieve socialism' (p. 60).

The actual acquiescence of the Conservative Party in the main features of Labour's programme clearly squares this circle. This acquiescence, first publicly noticed in the 1950s in the form of Butskellism, really dates back to the Baldwin and Chamberlain governments, which embarked on large social democratic projects, and on state ownership of selected industries, throughout the 1930s. This was their response to the growth of Labour as the major opposition, and its displacement of the Liberal Party. As the government embraced mild social democracy, its outriders went a good deal further. Harold Macmillan, in 1936, actually called for the creation of a centrist party, 'a fusion of all that is best of the left and the right', which he thought should be led by the Labour politician Herbert Morrison. Macmillan was then a nobody, probably only able to publish his dull and cumbersome social democratic book *The Middle Way* because of his family's control of a publishing firm. But the war, by greatly increasing state interference in the economy, would help to make him a very important somebody.

Macmillan was not, even then, as much of a dissenter from official Toryism as he seemed. British social services in 1939 were the most highly developed on the planet, after eight years of supposedly callous Tory and National government. This is not my assessment, but that of the historian Paul Addison. Addison concludes (*The Road to 1945*, Pimlico, London, rev. edn, 1994, p. 33):

> The social services of Britain, taken all in all, were the most advanced in the world in 1939, and the Social Democrats in Sweden, the Labour Party in New Zealand, and the New Deal Democrats in the United States, were trying to bring about many of the improvements which [British] Conservatism took for granted.

The semi-official 1939 film *The Lion has Wings*, made to inspire patriotism at home and sympathy abroad in the Phoney War period, while Neville Chamberlain was still Prime Minister, is startling in the way it highlights slum clearance, the building of new (and less authoritarian) schools, the introduction of statutory paid holidays and improved health care. The sunlit pictures of new blocks of workers' flats look like socialist or even Communist propaganda. There is a clear note of annoyance in the film – perhaps Neville Chamberlain's own feeling – that the sheer cost of war will interrupt all these costly social programmes. Mr Chamberlain need not have worried. The war's immense increase of state interference in the life of the nation moved what was already a strong social democratic consensus even more firmly to the Left and ensured that his social schemes were entrenched and greatly extended in the later 1940s. Had the Tories won the 1945 election, they would have moved in much the same direction as the Attlee government, though no doubt with some differences. As Addison remarks (p. 15), 'When Labour swept to victory in 1945, the new consensus fell, like a branch of ripe plums, into the lap of Mr Attlee.' That consensus had partly been created by the Tory Party.

The Tories, as is well known, decided after 1945 not to challenge even those parts of the Labour revolution with which they disagreed. Interested as always in office more than power, they took the view that quite enough of Conservative Britain survived, and would continue to survive, even after the Attlee revolution. They left most nationalised industries in state hands. They had, after all, nationalised a number of enterprises, including the National Grid and British Airways, before the war. They accepted the National Health Service. They even (though briefly) supported the creation of state secondary schools which were the equal of the independent sector.

The Harold Wilson governments of 1964–6 and 1966–70, with their high taxation and economic crises, and their increasing difficulties with the Trades Unions, kindled a sort of resistance in the Tory Party, which was tested by their unexpected and largely unexplained election victory in 1970.

Some of the statements made by the Edward Heath government early in its life, and many of the actions of the Tory government under Margaret Thatcher, seemed to challenge the 1945 social treaty. But there was less substance than there seemed to be in these challenges. Mr Heath was mostly concerned with entry to the Common Market, itself a fundamentally social democratic project. He was also unlucky, economically derailed by the 1973 oil crisis, compelled to nationalise Rolls Royce and maddened into unreason by coal strikes which he had no idea how to handle. Mrs Thatcher's rhetoric, like that of Mr Heath, was fiercer than her actions. She will almost certainly be seen by future historians as a less radical ruler than she appeared at the time – whereas Harold Wilson and Anthony Blair will be seen as more radical than they appeared. She did denationalise a number of industries, turning them instead into state-regulated monopolies which gave the government power over them, without responsibility for their failings. But she also nationalised local government and the English school system, and created a plethora of quangos which employed (and employ) large numbers of people, so leaving great multitudes as government employees, direct or indirect, and vast regions of the economy dependent on the state.

Simon Jenkins, in his *Thatcher and Sons* (London, Allen Lane, 2006) says that there is unquestionable continuity between Mrs Thatcher, Mr Blair and Mr Brown in such things. He uses this to support his (untypically conformist) belief in the conventional wisdom that New Labour is conservative in nature. But there is an equally plausible and opposite explanation, which is that the Thatcher government remained largely social democratic and Macmillanite despite its rhetoric, and that this allowed Labour to pursue an even more radically interventionist policy when it returned to power in 1997.

It was not specially difficult for 'New Labour' to accept the Thatcher changes, which left Britain with a public sector as powerful and as important as it had had at any time since 1945, and with an enormous welfare state. The Left were angry with Mrs Thatcher because of her unwillingness to *raise* spending on the NHS, though they pretended for propaganda purposes that she was imposing 'cuts'. They also rightly suspected her of a general hostility to the welfare state, though this dislike had little effect. They loathed her because of her apparent cultural conservatism, on education, sexual politics and patriotism – though these attitudes, too, turned out to be rather illusory on close examination. Where she tried to reform these things, she tended to get nowhere or even make them worse – especially in education where the main results of her government were the dismal National Curriculum and the severely devalued and egalitarian GCSE examination. But their principal quarrels were over the Cold War, and over her treatment of the unions, issues which were dead before she was forced from office.

Interestingly, her ejection came as a direct result of her only really dangerous departure from the consensus. This was her very late conversion to an anti-EU position after many years of keen support for the European project. The fashionable claim, that she was brought down by the Poll Tax, does not stand up to analysis. The crises which led to her departure were brought about by conflict with the pro-EU members of her government. First was the Westland affair, which had Europe at the bottom of it, and the dangerous resignation of Michael Heseltine, an enemy who could be neither co-opted nor crushed. Then she had her war with Geoffrey Howe and Nigel Lawson over the Exchange Rate Mechanism. After that she made her Bruges speech attacking European political integration and her declaration – the famous triple 'No!' in the Commons – that she would not accept the rule of EU courts and institutions over Britain. It was this which led to Geoffrey Howe's resignation and his bitter, merciless speech which was meant to bring her down, and duly did.

With Mrs Thatcher destroyed and her influence purged, with opposition to the EU reduced to a neutered and meaningless 'scepticism', and with the Tory Party clearly signalling, since 2001, its acceptance that it will not return to any part of Thatcherism, Labour can reasonably happily hand over office (but not power) to the Tory Party, confident that, when it eventually returns, its programme will not have been seriously disrupted, let alone reversed. The twenty-five years dreamed of by Aneurin Bevan have not quite come to pass. But there have been three revolutionary periods of Labour government. These were 1945–51, which created the welfare state and the NHS, neither of them reversible; 1964–70, which began and consolidated the cultural and moral revolution, turned the schools into egalitarian engines, and transformed the welfare state from a safety net into a powerful disincentive to unskilled work; and 1997–2010(?), which greatly extended the cultural and moral revolution, removed most conservative elements from the constitution, politicised the civil service, further expanded the public sector through the NHS and local government and broke up the United Kingdom.

The Tory Party's much longer periods in government in the same period did not lead to the reversal of these measures. The Tories were largely employed in winding up the British Empire which they had hitherto supported. This dreary process was the inevitable consequence of Britain's surrender in Singapore in 1942, but also the active policy of Labour. So it received no significant opposition. Even so, it involved the deliberate trampling on the dreams and loyalties of many of the Tories' own supporters. Those who were shocked by New Labour's crude suppression of the aged Leftist Walter Wolfgang, when he dared heckle the platform over the Iraq war, would do well to read accounts of the treatment of Empire Loyalists who tried to heckle the Tory Prime Minister, Harold Macmillan, at a Tory rally in Blackpool in October 1958. They objected both to Commonwealth immigration and to the winding up of the Empire. The fury with which they were driven from the hall made it plain that the Tory Party no longer wanted anything to do with such people or their opinions, which had been the private views of their own leadership only a decade before, as recently published archives on the Churchill government make clear (Cabinet papers, 3 February 1954, reported in *The Observer*, 5 August 2007). Reginald Bosanquet, then an Independent Television News reporter, witnessed the events. He subsequently told a court hearing (in May 1959) that the treatment of the hecklers was 'excessively violent'. Another distinguished journalist, Bernard Levin, also gave evidence of needless severity by stewards. He saw one of the hecklers marched into a room by uniformed attendants: 'I heard cries and the door was repeatedly banged from the other side. When he came out he was very distressed.' He was also bleeding heavily from the nose and his shirt was torn. The hecklers' own accounts of the incident, when they attempted to prosecute those involved, were even more lurid.

The Conservative Party, an organisation whose main purpose is to obtain office for its leading figures at almost any cost, and which is proud of its lack of any dogma, was not merely passively content to play its part in establishing the new Britain created after 1945. It was often actively enthusiastic about doing so. A parallel conflict, more gentlemanly but no less telling, came when Mr Macmillan decided to abandon Tory ideas of fiscal responsibility in January 1958. The Chancellor of the Exchequer, Peter Thorneycroft, and two Treasury Ministers, Enoch Powell and Nigel Birch, resigned in protest. Astonishingly, Mr Macmillan survived what would have been a fatal blow to most Prime Ministers, dismissing the mass walk-out of all his Treasury ministers as 'a little local difficulty'. The Labour Opposition could not take advantage of the division because it supported Macmillan. By governing as if he were a Labour premier, Macmillan was able to crush a powerful and economically expert section of his own ministry. This in many ways sums up the nature of 'Conservative' government during this period. Those Tories who were broadly social democratic or socially liberal in policies could and did work in concert with Labour to ensure that there was no going back on 1945 and that the Tories' own socially conservative supporters had little influence over legislation. A similar alliance would be used to open the way to the Chatterley Trial and the collapse of obscenity laws, through the Obscene Publications Act. The same contacts were effective in helping the 'Private Members' Bills' which created the permissive society. And another, similar cross-party alliance would eventually achieve the even more significant acceptance of Common Market membership.

Only one thing could have prevented the completion of this project – the collapse of the Tories and their replacement by a genuinely conservative political party uninterested in any such treaty with the Left, and willing to poach votes from Labour on a large scale through raising issues such as immigration and disorder, where working-class voters mistrusted their 'natural' party. This was a real possibility and one feared by Labour, which has always been nervous of and vulnerable on these issues. *It was greatly in Labour's interest, once the Tory Party had accepted so much of Labour's programme as unalterable, that the Tory Party should be preserved against the danger of dissolution.* It may even be the case that the more far-sighted Labour strategists privately accept that a period of Conservative government, under a leadership such as Mr Cameron's, which would not reverse New Labour's measures, is actually desirable.

Anyone who doubts the existence of this strange tenderness should read carefully the following remarks made by Peter Kellner, the former political journalist who is now head of the YouGov polling organisation. Mr Kellner was speaking at a gathering sponsored by the organisation Editorial Intelligence called 'Can Cameron Crack it?' (which took place on 20 June 2007, at the Royal Institute of British Architects, in Portland Place). Mr Kellner's connections to the Left-wing establishment are close and cordial. He has been a member of the Labour Party for more than three decades and is married to Baroness (Catherine) Ashton, for many years a Labour minister and valued member of the Labour establishment. At the time of her husband's remarks she was leader of the House of Lords and Lord President of the Council, and in October 2008 she was nominated to the European Commission by Gordon Brown.

I asked Mr Kellner why so many people in the establishment seemed anxious to pretend that the Tories are a serious force (which they then most certainly were not, as he had explained in detail with polling figures showing how far they were from a parliamentary majority). He replied: 'I think it's really important that the Conservative Party does survive as a substantial brand, because there will always be a need for a centre-right party.'

Mr Kellner read my mind and continued by answering the next question I had planned to ask:

> If the Conservatives were to go the way that Peter [Hitchens] expects – and I think possibly would relish – I am frightened as to what kind of right-of-centre politics would then spring up ...
>
> One of the great virtues of British politics ... is that we have not had a substantial far-right nationalist xenophobic party in Britain. A substantial Conservative Party is our best bulwark against the kind of politics that I think could become very nasty.

The exaggerated verbiage of 'far-right', 'xenophobic' and 'nationalist' is the sort of language which political figures of the self-described centre feel free to use about those outside their consensus. It is merely the jargon that such people in all three main parties use to categorise those who want to leave the European Union, those who oppose mass immigration and those who think that criminals should be punished rather than managed.

Mr Kellner is quite correct to see the Tory Party as the Left's best line of defence against the development of a party that might pursue radical objectives such as national independence and social conservatism. Nor do conformist conservatives find this role embarrassing or unwelcome. The Tory MP Edward Vaizey, who is a close adviser to Mr Cameron and who was sitting on the same platform, did not leap in to disavow Mr Kellner's endorsement.

Mr Kellner is not alone in his feelings. He is unusual only in his frankness. Labour ministers, and the national establishment as a whole, were greatly alarmed when the Tory Party began to disintegrate under the leadership of Iain Duncan Smith. They were much relieved by Michael Howard's disreputable putsch against Mr Smith, which in other circumstances they would have condemned.

The trouble was that Mr Smith did actually represent the force and mind of the Conservative Party at that time. That is why he became leader. He was a disastrous Leader of the Opposition because the Conservative Party was weak, divided and lacking in ideas, but also still held to an idea that it ought to be conservative, and to oppose a Labour government. The Howard coup d'état artificially avoided this problem. It took the Tory Party out of the hands of its members and placed it in a sort of trusteeship supported vigorously by certain newspapers which have become establishment organs, by the BBC and, indirectly, by the Labour government. This support was expressed in various ways: through the plentiful and prominent speculation which prepared the public for the coup; by the uncritical coverage of the event itself; by the failure of journalists to question Mr Howard in a hostile way, as they were entitled to do when an entire political party had overthrown its lawfully elected leader (who was also leader of Her Majesty's Opposition) in a backstairs plot. Mr Howard's occasionally despotic acts after his takeover, especially the arbitrary sacking of the Tory candidate Howard Flight, and an attempt to centralise the party organisation in ways until then unheard of, were not used to attack Mr Howard in any sustained way. Contrast the widespread acceptance of Mr Howard's unopposed election with the incessant sniping at Gordon Brown over his failure to secure a proper democratic mandate from his own party. There is no consistency. The difference must be explained by partiality.

But an essential (though unstated) part of the change was that the Tory Party should now cease to be conservative, or an opposition, but become a 'responsible', 'Centre-Left', alternative party of government. That is to say, it would have to obey Mr Blair's Wellingborough Decree.

The strange and new character of Mr Howard's leadership was emphasised by his action against Howard Flight. Mr Flight was an MP of some experience supported by his local Constituency Association. Mr Howard sacked him as if he were an employee (which he was not) for daring to make some conservative remarks in a speech to a private gathering. This could – and should – have been viewed as a demonstration of complete contempt for Parliament and for his own voters, just as his own seizure of the leadership was. But it was not. Mr Howard also narrowly failed to achieve a rule change which would have destroyed the traditional autonomy of Conservative Associations altogether. But he had already demonstrated, in the sacking of Mr Flight, that a central executive could and would over-ride the party whenever it chose, and would get away with it. The potent media, once again, stood aside and refrained from serious or sustained criticism. The Tory Party had been centralised, and the power of Associations to choose candidates or dissent from a powerful, wealthy central headquarters had been permanently weakened. In a two-party system such as ours, where the main parties, rather than the voters, are the gatekeepers of Parliament through the selection of candidates, this counts as a major constitutional reform. It also further diminishes the independence and standing of MPs and of Parliament as a whole, as it was intended to do.

Mr Cameron's media-led and media-created campaign for the Party leadership was made possible by Mr Howard and helped by him, especially in its timing. Mr Cameron's campaign faltered several times, but his media allies repeatedly renewed their support and were decisive in creating the impression that he was uniquely qualified, and that his rivals were incapable of winning wider electoral support. It is notable that an important media force, the *Spectator* magazine, gave its backing to Mr Cameron when he was still regarded as a minor candidate in the party. How and why did this come about? Coincidence theorists doubtless have their explanations. The rest of us may wonder if it was not agreed over lunch at some point.

The possibility that none of the candidates could win broad national favour, and that the Tory Party had ceased to be viable, was not discussed, though it is by no means impossible that this is so. In many ways, these media commentators were as powerful as the Trades Union block votes had once been in Labour leadership elections. Those who did not have this backing could do and say what they liked, but could not penetrate Mr Cameron's armour of media glamour. Mr Cameron could do what he liked – and in one televised clash with his main rival he was judged by many to have done poorly – but it still did not affect his standing.

Mr Cameron's election was followed by a number of autocratic measures, similar to Mr Howard's and having the same centralising purpose – particularly the attempted imposition of an 'A-list' of approved candidates. It was also followed by the extraordinary dismissal – for an offence he had not committed – of the shadow minister Patrick Mercer. Mr Mercer had made some truthful comments about racial bigotry in the army. He was falsely accused of expressing such bigotry and Mr Cameron dismissed him in a mobile telephone call, without a hearing or any sort of due process. Mr Cameron repeatedly made it clear that Conservative MPs were no longer free to speak in ways that had once been second nature to them. The rules which they had to observe brought them far closer in policy and in character to their supposed opponents on the Labour benches.

No Tory MP was ever disciplined for being too socio-logical about crime, for being too enthusiastic about high social spending, for praising comprehensive education, for favouring unlimited immigration or accelerated integration with the European Union. Mr Cameron broke a clear promise he had given to the 'Cornerstone' group of Tory MPs during his campaign – that he would withdraw the Conservative Party from a federalist EU political formation. But he was not tormented by the media for this breach of trust, since it was a breach of trust they approved of. Mr Cameron made deliberately provocative comments and speeches about many touchstone subjects, from global warming to homosexual civil partnership and 'hoodies' These were all carefully designed to demonstrate that he had been granted the power, by election and media canonisation, to take the Conservative Party sharply to the Left on social and cultural issues. They simultaneously humiliated the social conservatives in his party and exalted the social radicals. Those who seemed likely to oppose this, like Mr Mercer, were dealt with summarily. Their offence was to have committed the crime of conservative opinion, aggravated by news coverage. The road to a general de-conservatisation of the Tory Party, with the encouragement and permission of the media classes, was open. It was clear that it was the other direction which was closed.

There has always been a general belief in this country that there is little or no difference between the two major parties in the state, and it has always been partly true. But it has also until recently been significantly untrue. The two parties were separated by a large number of small but significant differences which added up to a major difference when they swapped sides in the Commons. But in the final years of this decade, it is true as it has never been before. The two parties, at their real centres, are now so close that the watcher is reminded of the moment at the end of *Animal Farm* when the animals gaze through the window, look from man to pig and from pig to man, and are no longer able to tell which is which. Their militant or principled wings, the Labour traditional Left and the Tory traditional Right, have never been so marginal or so quiet. It is as if the members of the old Tribune group and the Tory Cornerstone group are the only ones who have not grasped that their preoccupations no longer matter and the argument has moved elsewhere.

The two parties are so close that in April 2008, Mr Cameron felt able to heap public praise (in an interview with the *Daily Telegraph*) on three former or present Labour ministers, Alan Milburn, Stephen Byers and Andrew Adonis. A few days later, the Labour fundraiser Lord Levy disclosed that Anthony Blair did not believe that Gordon Brown could defeat Mr Cameron at the approaching election. This was not convincingly denied, and those schooled in politics recognised what it really meant – that Mr Blair does not think Mr Brown *should* defeat Mr Cameron. A few weeks later Michael Gove, the Shadow Education Secretary, referred to Alan Milburn as one of a number of 'impressive' Labour figures with whom Mr Brown could not work. He also quoted Mr Milburn's musings that it would now be almost impossible for him, a boy born on a council estate, to become a Cabinet Minister (considerably more impossible, as each year goes by, if British education policy proceeds in its current egalitarian direction). Not long afterwards, Mr Gove met Lord Levy, who had been Mr Blair's chief fundraiser but who made no secret of his scorn and dislike for Mr Brown. Mr Milburn suggested publicly that Mr Brown's handling of his office could cost him the next election.

These developments are part of the creation of a permanent government of the self-described 'centre', in which individuals as well as policies are interchangeable. They were the continuation of a process that began during the Major government, when a number of Tory MPs (for example, Alan Howarth and Shaun Woodward) defected directly to the Parliamentary Labour Party, in some cases to become ministers later. Such defections had until then been extremely rare, and usually involved fringe figures without hope of preferment. (A less significant defection, that of the

Tory MP Quentin Davies to Labour in 2007, was more typical of the old type. Mr Davies made a fool of himself by defecting in the wrong direction, rather like a man fleeing from West to East Germany in 1989.) They were also a continuation of the Labour media role in the Michael Howard putsch.

Now it is clear what the next stage will be. The electorate are to be allowed the semblance of change, while being denied its substance; at least if the voters can be lashed and hounded to the voting stations by the media in sufficient numbers, this is what will happen. If the plan works, the torch of New Labour is to be passed, over Mr Brown's frowning, puzzled head, directly from Mr Blair to Mr Cameron. The electorate are to be offered the opportunity to change the face of the government, but emphatically not to change its nature. Further, by winning the election, Mr Cameron will be able to crush, for the foreseeable future, the remaining moral, social and political conservatives in his party who are already pitifully weak. He will be able to claim (falsely, but who is paying attention?) that his party has failed to win three elections with 'Right-wing policies' but has finally triumphed under the banner of social liberalism and high public spending.

5

The Great Landslide:
New Labour's Loss of
the Media Classes

The role of the media in this business is astonishingly blatant. One curious feature of this multiple mutual crossover between supposed Right and alleged Left was particularly obvious in London during the 2008 contest for the capital's Mayoralty. Some prominent Left-wingers, notably the journalists Martin Bright, Andrew Gilligan and Nick Cohen, explicitly attacked the Labour Mayor, Ken Livingstone, despite the fact that this would materially help his Conservative challenger, Boris Johnson.

Mr Bright, Mr Gilligan and Mr Cohen must have known what the effect of their interventions would be. Mr Johnson was the only serious challenger to Mr Livingstone, and the most likely beneficiary if Mr Livingstone lost support. They raised perfectly legitimate complaints about Mr Livingstone's methods and beliefs. But these things had been well known to observers of London politics for many years, and it had never mattered before on the Left. Left-wing journalists had been ready to stay silent about them, or belittle them, rather than endanger one of their own.

The thing which had changed was that, for all these thoughtful Leftists, the idea of helping a Tory to win an election – if only indirectly, for none of them openly called for a Tory vote – was no longer a form of treason, repulsive and impossible. In a country with an adversarial two-party system, media commentators who are openly partisan are expected to remain on the side which they have adopted. This time they did not. Nor will they at the coming general election, where at the very least the Left's commentators will be far more critical of Mr Brown than they ever were of Mr Blair – and in some cases will openly sympathise with Mr Cameron. In the late summer of 2008, the *Guardian* newspaper published a series of articles sympathetic to Mr Cameron, an action which will make it easier for that newspaper to be at least equivocal when an election comes. This complete rule change in the way the Fourth Estate chooses and announces its allegiances is once again, a major undiscussed constitutional upheaval.

The preparation for a shift at the general election began at about the same time as the assaults on Mr Livingstone. Attacks on Mr Brown, deeply personal and unceasing, came far more intensely from newspapers and commentators which had previously been warm supporters of Mr Blair, than from those which had been generally conservative. *The Times*, which has never been more of an establishment paper than it is under its present ownership, is always a reliable guide to the very heart and centre of conventional wisdom and received opinion. It had been one of the most slavish supporters of New Labour in its early years. It now began to run cartoons and news stories which constantly stressed the problems of Mr Brown, and made him look foolish and rudderless. In fact, during this strange period of political confusion in April 2008, one of the most cogent and powerful defences of Mr Brown came from Peter Oborne, the conservative columnist of the conservative *Daily Mail*, but – unusually in his generation or his trade – a gentleman of independent mind, who had often stood up to the Blairist herd mentality of the political correspondents. Alas, Mr Oborne could not keep it up for long, and a few weeks later was borne away by the bleating flock into a renewed endorsement of Mr Cameron.

For some months before this outbreak, the BBC had also been noticeably fairer to the Conservative Party, and readier to carry criticism of the government, than at any time for many years.

These extraordinary developments, far more interesting than volumes of the Westminster lunch-table gossip which passes as political reporting in most of the British media, went largely unnoticed by the journalistic armies assigned to Westminster. Consumers of newspapers and news bulletins are extraordinarily unaware of the way in which some facts qualify as 'stories' and are given sustained prominence (as explained by Peter Oborne in the extract above), and others go almost completely unnoticed.

How have we reached this strange place, where Left-wing journalists and Labour politicians are doing all they can to assure the defeat of the Labour Party at local (and I predict, before long, general) elections? Why have the great political tides, which once swept governments in and out, ceased to ebb and flow? Why are the most significant events of recent British history all in the form of coups and putsches supported by the media – the Tory overthrow of Margaret Thatcher and, later, of Iain Duncan Smith; the takeover of the Labour Party by the Blair faction, and the subsequent evisceration of the organisation to the point where its conference was a powerless backdrop to a speech from the leader.

Is there any alternative to the non-politics of personal attack, image and alleged competence, which has now replaced the centuries-old adversarial system? What explains the slow strangulation of that system? Have Left and Right ceased to exist? Or have they moved their encampments elsewhere? Is the entire country in fact cradled in a comfortable consensus about everything from social security to sex education? Who are the establishment now? Why has the compass ceased to work, which once reliably told us who was where and which side they were on?

That is what I hope to explore in this book.

Part II

The Left Escapes to the West

6

Riding the Prague Tram

You cannot do it now, but I passed many times beneath the scowling gateways that took you through the Iron Curtain. My first such journey was to Prague in 1978. We (the future Mrs Hitchens and I) had been urged to go there by a veteran Communist, once a secret carrier of gold and messages for Stalin's Kremlin. She had said that Prague, then visited by almost nobody in the West, was incomparably the loveliest city on the continent, and the only one surviving where one might still breathe the atmosphere of Europe before the great destruction of 1939–45. This friend had been supplied by her Communist superiors with couture clothes and put up in the best hotels so as to attract less attention, and so had seen the city at its most splendid.

We crossed the line just outside a place called Schirnding, in a somnolent corner of Franconia. They took the big, fat, smart West German locomotive off the train and a small, meagre, dirty diesel, that had once been red, crept smokily over from the sad Czech lands to replace it. We rolled a little way into a treeless zone of rusty barbed wire and weedy gravel, then halted. We were at last 'over there'. All of a sudden sour, wiry men in scuffed boots and creased, dispiriting grey uniforms climbed into the coaches and swarmed over and under the train, and then inside it. Our British passports made us immune from their prying hands, but did not spare us the sight, or the sensation, of insulting totalitarian intrusiveness and contempt for private life. The Czechs beside us were searched to their bones and their fillings, and submitted without so much as rolling their eyes. It was their passive surrender that was most telling and disturbing. The red stars decorating the compartment had seemed a joke, a few hours back in comfortable, jolly Nuremberg with its sausages and gingerbread and air of cheery prosperity and post-Nazi niceness. Now they didn't seem amusing or ironic at all.

As the light slowly thickened we penetrated deeper and deeper into another, opposite world. We pressed our noses against the windowpane as we trundled through a planet we had imagined but never seen. Look! They really do have huge red banners with slogans on them, draped across the squares. Look! The shop windows actually are inadequately furnished with wonky consumer goods in unpleasant colours or dowdy packaging. Look! They really do have stainless steel teeth. Look! Their clothes really are uniform and shabby, their faces are closed, they walk and stand differently from us, they have to loiter in long queues and ride in ancient trams – not because it is picturesque to do so but because it is the only way home. As for home, it is not private or safe when you eventually get there, bone weary with your shabby string bag of sub-standard groceries, exhausted vegetables, fat pork and dense bread. Running into Prague in the twilight, we began to see great rows of Soviet railway carriages, decorated with the hammer and sickle. We had passed into the gravitational pull of Moscow's dark sun. As we left the train I cast an eye at the departure board above the platforms. Not one Western destination was mentioned. It was, as promised, another world.

That night we also discovered that they really did live in fear of the secret police. After a beery supper with a Czech acquaintance we had begun to feel foolishly relaxed. I mentioned a political subject as our tram bucked down Wenceslas Square. 'Shut up!' hissed our friend. 'Don't you realise where you are?' And, all of a sudden, I did realise where we were. I recalled the old joke about Jan Masaryk, beloved hero of Czech nationalism, being asked in the closing months of World War II what his war aims were. 'My war aims?' he replied. 'I want to go home. I want to ride in a tram down Wenceslas Square and I want to be able to say (and here he adopted a querulous old man's voice) "I don't think much of the present government".' Masaryk did eventually go home and was soon afterwards murdered, for not thinking much of the present government. A whole series of bricks, long loosened, fell from a wall in my mind. This was not a movie or a thriller. This was life in an advanced and orderly European capital, among educated and civilised men and women, in one of the most beautiful cities in the world. Speech was not free. That was what these words meant. I was genuinely afraid of authority for the first time since my years at a strict-regime preparatory school, on the edge of Dartmoor, in the lost, stern days before Harold Wilson, decimal coinage and Nuffield maths. The following day I almost leaped from my skin when, on another tram, I was confronted by a hard-looking, flat-featured man who flashed a red-and-gold metal badge in my face and spoke brusquely to me. For a long moment I had visions of disagreeable cellar interrogations and plaintive attempts to contact the British Embassy. As it happened, he turned out to be the ticket inspector. The problem was, he might easily have been someone altogether more disturbing.

So, in Prague, began the serious part of my education, most of it provided by what might be called the University of Fleet Street. My official university years had been spent as a full-time Trotskyist, attempting to stir the working class into revolution. I learned much from this, though I did not realise it at the time because I was trying mainly to absorb as much Marxist piffle as possible and was paying little conscious attention to the important things of life. Sometimes our efforts to suck up to militant Trade Unionists and to fight the fascist menace at the same time got a little mixed up with each other. I still recall with hot shame an October 1972 harangue at a York University

Students' Union meeting, in which I tried and failed to link a
dock strike and our plans to oppose a National Front march
in Leicester. As I floundered dialectically in the crowded dining
hall, a cruel voice called out 'There aren't any docks in
Leicester!'

I was (rightly) laughed off the stage, an experience much
worse than it sounds. But I am not sorry about our obsession
with the working class. My sect's dogged pursuit of real
industrial workers gave me the sort of contact with such
people that my generation of the middle class normally did
not get – since we were too late for National Service.

Hospitable, and touched by what they saw as our real
concern for their welfare, bus conductors, coachbuilders,
steelworkers, dustmen, railwaymen, dockers and
coalminers took us into their homes, bought us drinks,
introduced us to their families, explained the details of
their lives and their work, indulged our ignorance, treated
us unreservedly as friends and equals. This was and is
shaming. We wished to use them. We had been taught to
think of them as an undifferentiated class, a mighty force
rolling up their sleeves over their beefy forearms as they
advanced into the future under our wise leadership. We
found out that they were not a 'class' but individuals with
lives as rich and complex as our own, if not more so, and
also that they were above all our fellow countrymen, who
hated any slights against their own nation. I learned in the
end that they did not much want to be led, or if they did,
they did not want to be led by people like me, or to where
we thought they wanted to go.

I am asked so often about my change of mind, my
defection from the Left, that I think it worth giving a brief
description of it here. It was not a swift revelation, as so
many unreconstructed Leftists would like it to be. There
was nothing pathological or Pauline about it. What
happened to me could happen to anyone with Left-wing
opinions, which is why I sometimes think my very existence
is an irritant to readers of the *Guardian*, and why such

people hope that my change of mind resulted from some sort of brainstorm or trauma – one unlikely to happen to them. As it happens, what happened to me is unlikely to happen to most of them because they are so very afraid of it, and so not adventurous enough to take the necessary risks, poor things.

There was no blinding light, no sudden moment of realisation. Two different sets of experience, grinding away like twin millstones, brought it about during several years. It took me from 1968 to 1975 to work out that revolutionary Marxism had been a failure in the past and might be a danger in the future. By 1978 I had made my way as far as the Hampstead Constituency Labour Party, but I found myself in a besieged and despised minority. This was because I was by then a convinced supporter of nuclear deterrence and the monarchy and an opponent of Irish Republican terrorism. I had reached these positions exactly because I was a former Leninist, and so wholly unsentimental about my political choices. If I no longer believed in socialist revolution, but instead supported the freedom and independence of my own country, then we obviously needed our own bomb. Irish terrorists were plainly an enemy to be crushed (proper Marxists loathe terrorism anyway). The monarchy clearly strengthened our free constitution and formed a potent barrier against fascistic movements by keeping politicians away from grandeur and worship. What was the problem for the other comrades? Alas, they *were* sentimentalists, and so uninterested in the iron logic of practicality. One Irish rebel song, one showing of that absurd, unrealistic film *The War Game*, one spasm of reflex class-war republicanism, and they were lost to reason.

I left Labour in 1984 because I had become a political reporter and didn't think I should be a party member, though I had become pretty tired of being called to order for 'provoking hecklers' during my own speeches at the Hampstead General Management Committee. This body met in the Edwardian majesty of Sir Thomas Beecham's old Hampstead home, then as now the headquarters of the train drivers' union ASLEF. This sort of chairmanship, which didn't even pretend to be fair, convinced me I was not dealing with an open-minded organisation. So I ended my formal links with the Labour Party. But if I am honest it wasn't quite over yet. During the Thatcher years I felt a great deal of sympathy with the Social Democratic Party who, like me, wanted to salvage something from the mastless hulk of democratic socialism, and who instinctively disliked the shark-like figures who gathered, jaws snapping, in the wake of Margaret Thatcher. I would say now that I reluctantly ceased to be a social democrat of any kind some time after the day in the autumn of 1990 when I became a registered resident of No 26 Kutuzovsky Prospekt, Moscow. The Brezhnev family were my close neighbours and 'real existing socialism' was crumbling to grey dust all round me. In this vast wreck, I saw too many echoes of my old political aims, and of their unintended consequences. I resolved to have more modest political objectives in future.

The first millstone was my disillusionment with the people and institutions of the British Left, as I grew to know them from personal experience. The second was my increasing knowledge of the socialist countries of Eastern Europe, my dislike of what I found there and the growing conviction that it was the result of the same thinking to be found in the supposedly democratic parties of the Western Left. Of course it was different in local character, in the speed with which it had been done, the absolute power of those who had done it and the much greater wealth of Western societies. But it was, in truth, the same thing and it tended towards the same sad, undesirable end. For some time, thanks to the writings of Arthur Koestler, I persuaded myself that an honourable social democratic position existed, hostile to totalitarian Communism, wedded to freedom, and capable of achieving civilised and humane reforms. Inch by inch, I found I had to abandon this view as unworldly. It seemed to me that the destination of the civilised social democrats – even if they did not intend it – was the totalitarianism I loathed.

What I found in the concrete estates and the propaganda of the Warsaw Pact countries was worryingly close to what I could easily see in the greyer, harsher parts of my own country which – as a tyro revolutionary – I had often visited. Acquaintances in Communist Prague had urged me to explore the suburb of Karlin to see how dismal were the results of egalitarian communism. I expected to be shocked but found in Karlin (as I would later find in Warsaw's Praga, in East Berlin's Marzahn and in most of Moscow) something remarkably similar to the gigantic housing projects of dozens of Labour local authorities all over Britain. Where they had power to do so, they did the same.

Malcolm Muggeridge had long ago seen a startling similarity between Communists using power and Fabians seeking it, when he had mused that many of his 1920s Fabian acquaintances rather envied the Soviet Union's ability to make annoying opponents 'disappear'. His suspicions were confirmed when Beatrice and Sidney Webb (like many other Fabians, but more explicitly) declared Stalin's vast suburb of hell to be a 'new civilisation'. First they did this with a question mark. Then they abandoned the question mark. By the time it became clear to the slowest intelligence that the 'new civilisation' was a Pharaonic tyranny from mankind's cruel past, it was too late to retract, or even to replace the question mark. But the worst was known to the Webbs anyway, and they did not really mind. Muggeridge knew the Webbs well because he was married to their niece. He recalled in 'Many Winters ago in Moscow' (reprinted in *Tread Softly, for You Tread on My Jokes*, Fontana, 1968, p. 30):

What they (Beatrice and Sidney Webb) really admired was the regime's sheer power; the fact that there were no votes to be taken, no motions to be referred back, no tedious bone-headed trade unionists to be coaxed and cajoled. This emerged when Mrs Webb said: 'It's true that in the Soviet Union people disappear.' She accentuated this last word, '*disappear*,' and I realised, even in my

somewhat euphoric condition, how happy she would have
been if similar arrangements prevailed in the LCC (London
County Council) and recalcitrant councillors and aldermen
could be made likewise to disappear.

This encounter took place in 1932, just as Muggeridge was
about to leave for Moscow to take up a post as the correspondent there for the *Manchester Guardian*. There he would
encounter the man-made famine in the Ukraine, caused by
forced collectivisation. He would also see how much of the
world would refuse to acknowledge that it was even
happening, and how some journalists would work to suppress
or minimise the truth.

Muggeridge remarked in the same essay that the Webbs
had disliked the Bolsheviks in their early, revolutionary phase
but had come to admire them 'when Stalin and the GPU had
fully taken over, keeping the firing-squads busy and the labour
camps full' (ibid., p. 23).

The 1970s dogmatists of London local government were
only separated from their brethren in Prague, East Berlin
and Warsaw by the chance that had put them on the Western
side of the finish line when World War II ended. Does this
mean that they too would have supported the suppression of
opposition parties, the secret police and the Gulag, in their
own countries? We have only clues. One of them is that
figures much admired as 'decent' Bolsheviks by the Western
Left are in fact implicated in terrible repression. Nikolai
Bukharin, the 'darling of the Party', was eventually destroyed
in a hideous show trial. But he had himself taken a large part
in the similar show trials of leaders of the Russian Social
Revolutionary Party, and was destroyed by methods he had
himself used against others.

Another clue is the continuing effort by Western Leftists,
even nowadays, to make excuses for Vladimir Lenin (see
below) and to pin the blame for the perversion of the Russian
Revolution on Stalin. The older ones, of course, spent much
of their time actively defending Stalin, though it is now

considered rather bad form to mention this. But the attempt to launder Lenin simply does not fit with the historical facts. Why do they so dislike the truth, that Lenin was the exemplar for and the prototype of Stalin? It is tempting to suspect that they do not like the truth about themselves.

The third – and rather amusing – clue is the remarkable 'Stalinbad' industry that has arisen, but only since the USSR finally collapsed. This consists of increasing numbers of books, fiction and non-fiction describing the wickedness of the deceased Soviet leader. This new enterprise only really got into its stride in the late 1990s, almost fifty years after Stalin's death and his official denunciation in the USSR itself. So slow and cautious has the Western re-evaluation of Stalin been that I feel a growing admiration for Nikita Krushchev for so thoroughly dethroning his old chief in the 1956 Secret Speech. That speech was plainly as unwelcome to many Western Leftists as it was to the Communist loyalists in the Kremlin. The Western Leftists, living at a distance from the truth and having more need to deny it, maintained their illusions far longer than the old Soviet Communists did.

Mass-market books denouncing Lenin as the almost unhinged political killer which he actually was, screaming in a spittle-flecked rage for the mass executions of opponents, have yet to be written, and probably would not find a market among British book buyers, who continue to sentimentalise this appalling man and to romanticise the Soviet catastrophe. Young men and women who would choke rather than wear Nazi regalia still don garments bearing Soviet emblems, and representatives at the Tory Party conference in Birmingham in 2008 found themselves drinking in an expensive hotel bar called 'Pravda'. Who would drink in a bar called 'Der Stürmer'?

This self-delusion is even more the case with Trotsky, whose bloodstained intolerance is generally passed over because the 1960s student generation pretended then, and pretends still, that Trotsky was in some way a freedom-loving, Gulag-free alternative to Stalin. The truth (which I remember trying to wriggle out of in my Trotskyist days) is that Trotsky proved himself a mass murderer and tyrant at Kronstadt. We used to argue that the victims of that massacre were not proper Bolsheviks. We were as bad as the Stalin apologists and in many cases we still are. Trotsky would have purged, but perhaps more rationally than Stalin, and was not – being Jewish – a Judophobe like Stalin. He was undeniably a talented journalist. But he never had the chance to show his paces as a mass-murdering tyrant, only because he was a poor conspirator, bad at the office politics at which Stalin excelled.

It is interesting to set the new Stalinbad industry next to the parallel Hitler industry. This has been flourishing ever since 1945 and shows no signs of losing its power to sell books and inspire TV series and films. Compare the publishing and entertainment industry's response to the known facts about the Gulag. While the USSR still existed, Robert Conquest's *Great Terror* remained for many years the only work on this subject produced by a British writer of any standing, and he was not popular with the intellectual establishment for having written it. Alexander Solzhenitsyn's *Gulag Archipelago* had a brief effect but is now curiously forgotten, as is its author. There is no equivalent of the colossal industry devoted to examining and re-examining the Nazi concentration camps.

Solzhenitsyn was never fully welcomed into the West, where his religious, patriotic conservatism was seen as suspect and there were endless whispers alleging that he was anti-Semitic. Realising this, Solzhenitsyn treated his exile in Vermont as just that – exile – and never fitted comfortably into the spectrum of Western politics or thought. Neither he nor Andrei Sakharov – though both were self-sacrificial and peaceful resisters against a monstrous tyranny – have ever achieved anything like the standing obtained by Nelson Mandela, whose record is not quite so clean and who refused to denounce the violence of his comrades. Nor has Václav Havel, or Lech Wałęsa, or the forgotten Robert

Havemann. Nobody has heard of Fang Lizhi, and few in the West even know that the Chinese Gulag exists or what it is called ('Laogai'). And this is in spite of the fact that Mr Mandela's record is more ambiguous than any of theirs, and it is hard to claim that the apartheid state was any more evil than the Soviet Union, the Warsaw Pact tyrannies or Communist China, which may have ceased to be Communist but remains a frightening police state. Mr Mandela's advantage comes from having been the figurehead of a movement of the Left, significantly connected to (and in some important ways tainted by) a particularly slavish type of Stalinist Communism. The South African Communist Party could always be relied upon to endorse invasions and repressions by the USSR, which European Communists refused to support.

Communism, and Communist sympathy, remained academically and politically respectable in a way that National Socialism, Fascism and Falangism were not. The historian Eric Hobsbawm is a fine writer and a perceptive analyst. But if he were a persuasive apologist for the Third Reich, rather than for Communism, his abilities would not save him from obscurity or scorn. David Irving, an apologist for the Third Reich, is plainly not Hobsbawm's equal as a historian. But if he were, would he have been treated any better than he has been? Could Alan Bennett have written – let alone had produced and transmitted on a major national station – a successful TV play sympathising with a traitor (say, John Amery or William Joyce) who gave his services to National Socialist Germany? Of course not, and in my view rightly so. But it was perfectly possible for him to have a lasting success with *An Englishman Abroad*, which was needlessly kind to the personally repulsive and morally corrupt Communist traitor Guy Burgess. This play is treated as a sort of classic and was much praised by critics who would have choked rather than praise a parallel play (however witty) giving a sympathetic portrayal of Lord Haw Haw.

Unlike many conservatives, I do not view Leftism as dishonourable or deliberately evil. On the contrary, I respect its impulses and wish they led where they seek to go. I reject them because they lead somewhere entirely different, and rather unpleasant. But the Left simply will not see that the problems of socialism might be their fault. They will take credit for its acts of nobility and sacrifice, for the times when it has been right and everyone else wrong. I have heard the US Communist Party, that sink of Stalinism and treachery, defended on the grounds that it opposed the colour bar in the American South. No doubt it did, while simultaneously defending or denying the barbarities of Josef Stalin, who deported whole nations and was a gross Judophobe, planning a purge of Jews at the very end of his life, which was only prevented by his death. This would seem to suggest that its opposition to Southern racial bigotry was opportunist rather than principled.

But the Left will also not accept the blame for what its comrades do in power, their repeated tendency to attack liberty, their hostility to private life and their utter intolerance of criticism. The problem is that, if they recognise these things as essential results of their creed, they will have to abandon the Left, which is their home, their meat and drink, their family, their faith and their hope. That is so difficult that for most of them it is unthinkable. So instead they look for ways to help them escape from the unkind logic of their plight. The Iron Curtain was very useful to them, because they could claim to themselves and their opponents that they had nothing in common with what went on beyond it. They, after all, were not Bolsheviks or Russians. They had not had to cope with foreign interventions or a long civil war or an invasion by the Third Reich. All these excuses were true, but they were not a truthful answer to the charge levelled against them. The fault of the Western Left was that they willingly made excuses for repression when they were free not to make those excuses, and that they stayed silent about abuses when they were free to attack them.

The existence of the Iron Curtain also compelled the creation of reformed social democratic parties, especially in West Germany, which tried to maintain that their beliefs were now wholly compatible with capitalism and the nation state – and completely hostile to the systems on the far side of the frontier. The conversion was false. They were dissembling. Before the fall of the Iron Curtain, Western Leftists had been quite happy to defend the USSR from the very beginning. This can be seen in the many admiring travelogues and studies produced by 'democratic' Leftists and Fabians in the 1920s and 1930s. Even when these were written, refugee accounts were already exposing the barbarity of the Stalin state. These writers are well described in David Caute's *The Fellow Travellers* and also in Malcolm Muggeridge's autobiography *Chronicles of Wasted Time*.

After 1945, it was important for those socialists to maintain that the Marxist class conflict was over, so that they could take part in governing the world created by Marshall Aid. This was specially the case with the German Social Democrats, whose 1959 Godesberg programme had been portrayed as a final break with the Marxism of the party's past. Yet even after 1945 and the crushing of the East German workers' uprising in 1953, even after the Soviet invasion of Hungary in 1956 and of Czechoslovakia in 1968, Western European social democracy was still not wholly reconciled to capitalism or entirely finished with its flirtation with the USSR. Socialist parties across Europe would demonstrate this in the crisis over medium-range nuclear missiles in the 1980s. The campaign to prevent the deployment of Cruise and Pershing II weapons very nearly split even the German Social Democrats (SPD). Not long before this, West German Social Democrats would view the workers' movement of Poland as a risk to their improving relations with East Germany's Communist state. Moscow had intended to split the Western European Left, when it began targeting its own SS-20 rockets on European cities. Some thought the rockets were really aimed at the heart of the SPD. The ploy very nearly succeeded.

West Germans were specially afraid of a real war in Europe, having painfully rebuilt their country after the near-annihilation of much of the country in the later stages of World War II. They were conscious that such a war would be fought on their territory. There was also a submerged but definite sympathy between the peoples of West and East Germany, a desire for something approaching reunification. The SPD Chancellor, Willy Brandt, was a man much further to the Left than he stated publicly, and there is no doubt that his attempt to carve a separate Eastern policy was partly driven by this. In the meantime, almost all the major dissenters in East Germany were not Reaganites or Thatcherites, but independent socialists such as Robert Havemann, Rudolf Bahro, Wolf Biermann and Baerbel Bohley. The reunification they hoped for was not by any means the smashing victory for NATO and the free market which eventually came about. The recent history and unalterable geography of Germany, plus the existence of such an opposition in the East, made it difficult for Western Social Democrats, whose origins were in the same nineteenth-century movement, to view East Germany, or the Soviet bloc as a whole, in a straightforward Cold War 'them versus us' way.

Brandt's successor, the more conventional reformist socialist Helmut Schmidt, still continued the rapprochement with the East, which greatly improved the lives of many East Germans by allowing them closer links with families in the West, eased travel of West Germans to the East, poured large amounts of Western money into the East and brought about the release – by purchase – of many political prisoners.

The price of this relaxation was a very special relationship, which amounted to full diplomatic recognition, a state of affairs which would cause trouble years later, when a unified German government tried to prosecute former East German officials and politicians for shootings on the Inner-German border and other actions. And it was clear that the German government, and probably the voters too, had some difficulty when this relationship got in the way of the general Cold War struggle against Soviet tyranny.

A now-forgotten instance of this dilemma occurred on 13 December 1981, when the Polish Communist leader, General Wojciech Jaruzelski, declared a State of Emergency. This was an attempt to suppress the Solidarity movement, by then posing a serious threat to the rule of Communism. Many Solidarity activists were rounded up and imprisoned, and highly repressive measures were imposed on the country.

When the announcement was made, Helmut Schmidt was faced with an awkward choice. He was at the time on the eastern side of the Iron Curtain, at Gustrow, less than 100 miles from the Polish frontier. He was taking part in an East–West German summit with the East German Communist leader Erich Honecker. Honecker, who had been greatly disturbed by the unchecked unrest on his eastern frontier, would almost certainly have been consulted about the State of Emergency, along with other Warsaw Pact leaders, and must have approved of it.

The meeting was approaching its close and it would have been simple for Schmidt to have curtailed it and left abruptly, so marking his disapproval of the Polish repression. But he continued the talks until their prearranged end. The German to German rapprochement was more important to him than the liberty of Poland.

Into the midst of all these delicate complexities came a development which, on the face of it, made a war on German territory more likely, and more likely to be utterly devastating.

The gigantic group of Soviet Forces in Germany (GSFG) would have squashed the conventional forces of NATO had it ever been ordered into battle. NATO's troops, for political reasons, were in the wrong place (the most powerful American armies, confined to the US zone of occupation, did not face the most powerful Soviet divisions, and coordination between NATO armies was poor – they had, after much painful negotiation, managed to standardise their aircraft passenger sickbags, but little else).

But for many years this imbalance had been corrected by NATO's possession of tactical nuclear weapons. In theory,

NATO's willingness to use these to destroy Soviet military formations and supplies meant that an advance by Warsaw Pact conventional troops would swiftly trigger a nuclear war, since the only practical nuclear Soviet response would be the use of long-range missiles, which would inevitably provoke American retaliation and so bring about World War III. Such a nuclear war would destroy the Soviet homeland and the continental United States. Therefore no Soviet leader would give the order to advance. As a result, the Soviet conventional forces had no serious diplomatic impact on central Europe. NATO countries felt free to exist as they chose on their side of a frozen border. They in turn accepted that the peoples of the Warsaw Pact countries had to suffer Communist rule – hence NATO's complete inaction over the 1953 crushing of the East Berlin workers' rising, the 1956 Hungarian rising and the 1968 'Prague Spring'.

The position of Finland, not part of NATO but next to a Soviet frontier, was wholly different. Finland's foreign policy was strictly neutral, criticism of the Soviet Union muted or self-censored, and cabinet appointments in Finnish governments had (confidentially) to be approved by the Soviet Politburo. This arrangement would have been much more stringent had Finland not been part of a prosperous, confident and free Western European landmass. The threat of 'Finlandisation' was specially discussed in Germany. Stalin had long ago offered German unification in return for neutrality in March 1952 – an offer widely regarded as a cynical ploy, and dismissed on those grounds at the time. But Moscow, through its control of East Germany, alone had the power to allow unity on its own terms. This unstated fact was a feature of all negotiations between the USSR and NATO, and West German neutrality, or detachment of West Germany from NATO, remained a target of Soviet diplomacy until the Cold War was clearly lost. The Polish-sponsored Rapacki Plan of 1957, which would have included West Germany in a 'nuclear free zone', was a subtler attempt to gain the same end. Russian efforts to detach Germany from the rest of Europe were nothing new, as the

1922 Rapallo Pact between the Soviet Union and Weimar Germany, and the 1939 Stalin–Hitler Pact, showed.

The deployment of Soviet SS-20 Pioneer missiles from 1975 upset the old calculations. These rockets could only strike targets in Europe. Their launch – in response to the use of tactical nuclear weapons by NATO – could only be countered by a strategic counterstrike by the USA. But the USA might not be willing to use its Intercontinental Missiles in response to a purely European threat. Thus, the SS-20s made a limited European nuclear war possible, and so made a conventional war more thinkable. If war broke out, the strategic interests of the USA and the national interests of Germany might sharply diverge. If these SS-20 missiles were not countered by matching medium-range Western weapons, the Soviet armies in Europe could once again become a real threat West of the Iron Curtain. The pressure on Germany to become neutral – so destroying NATO – would increase relentlessly.

Soviet propaganda and negotiating techniques, in the years that followed, had many willing dupes in the Western countries. In Britain, the plan to counter the SS-20s with cruise missiles (and in Germany, Pershing-2 weapons) was falsely portrayed by the Left (who in my experience believed their own propaganda) as an aggressive move rather than as a response to an aggressive move. People who did not in any way regard themselves as pro-Soviet, or as apologists for the Soviet state, nonetheless did the Kremlin's work for it on demonstrations, in newspaper articles, TV programmes and Parliamentary debates.

The traditional British Left was both anti-American and sentimentally indulgent to the USSR. Presumably many of its more thoughtful members actually liked the idea of a Europe in which the USSR was the only nuclear power. That, after all, was what they campaigned for. But in Britain, where the Cold War was an extension of World War II and pacifism was seen as definitively unpatriotic, the anti-cruise movement was limited to the Left, an asset to the Conservatives and a disadvantage to the Labour Party.

Matters in Germany, as explained above, were by no means so simple. The country's neutralist, anti-war tendencies were much more serious and deeper-rooted than those in Britain, and in a way more politically respectable. And it was Helmut Schmidt, keenly conscious of this while at the same time a serious democrat and pro-NATO figure, who argued strongly for the 'double track' negotiations, in which NATO prepared to deploy cruise and Pershing-2 missiles, while negotiating for the removal of both.

Had those negotiations been badly handled, so that the NATO leadership had to take the blame for their failure, the extraordinary collapse of Soviet power which took place in the late 1980s might never have happened. The burden on the leadership of West Germany, and especially on its Social Democrats, was very heavy indeed.

Some of the more honest Western Leftists were willing to admit that they had things in common with their brethren in what many of them called 'the socialist countries'. Jonathan Steele, a first-rate foreign correspondent whose later work in the USSR was exemplary, courageous and enterprising, had earlier written a sympathetic book about East Germany, *Socialism with a German Face*, in which he had correctly identified the many things that a London Left-winger of the 1970s and early 1980s might like about the German Democratic Republic. And in truth he had an important point. As a bemused world found when the Berlin Wall collapsed, a surprising number of people in East Germany longed for it to be put back up again. On a recent visit to Halle Neustadt, a colossal 1960s concrete city of uniform blocks, mostly now demolished, I found sizeable colonies of elderly nostalgists dwelling among the ruins and rubble, still touchingly upholding what they regarded as the standards of the old East Germany, not least the 'human solidarity' which ethical Communists prize so highly.

But I also remember the same Jonathan Steele, the day after Soviet forces had committed atrocities against

Lithuanian nationalists in Vilnius in January 1991, barely containing his scornful fury while questioning (in fluent Russian) a sheepish colonel, spokesman for the Moscow military authorities. All the Western journalists there were enraged and exhausted – and in some cases (certainly mine) afraid. We had spent the night seeking sleep on the floors of hospitable Lithuanians, having stayed away from our hotels to avoid a rumoured mass arrest and deportation. What we had seen was mostly unnoticed in the West because the first stages of the recapture of Kuwait had captured the TV news and the newspaper front pages.

It had begun during a press conference called by Lithuania's new government. They had very recently declared independence, to the fury of the supposedly liberal Mr Gorbachev – who believed that the three tiny Baltic countries were indispensable to the defence of Leningrad, and to the Soviet economy (those who have since persuaded these states to join NATO should be aware that this belief still persists strongly among Russian elite conservatives). A young man came, shouting, into the press conference to say that there was shooting outside the press building, headquarters of all Lithuania's newspapers.

We hurried there, in my case praying under my breath. I did not fancy myself as a war correspondent. I have a morbid horror of lying in some insanitary, rudimentary hospital, groaning my life away in either great heat or frozen cold, having stopped a bullet in the gut, in the cause of writing a story for the foreign page. I have no idea if I could die for my country if called upon to do so, but I am absolutely sure that I do not wish to die for any newspaper, commemorated by a blurred picture and an inaccurate brief obituary.

I had never imagined that the collapse of the USSR would lead to real bloodshed, since its authority had crumbled so softly in Budapest, East Berlin and Prague. The violence in Romania had seemed exceptional (and exaggerated), having more to do with Nicolae Ceauşescu's old-fashioned autocratic behaviour than with Moscow. So this was something of a shock. Was my Moscow assignment to become a tour of small, savage wars as the many pieces of Stalin's empire tore themselves free? It looked horribly as if it might. As we approached the building we could hear the noise of gunfire, which does indeed sound like an enormous piece of cotton cloth being ripped by a giant hand, as the books say it does. It was very cold. We arrived to find that one man had had an eye casually shot from his head after a Soviet officer had hosed the front of the building with his sub-machine-gun, presumably to emphasise his authority.

Undeterred by this miserable piece of armed spite, a defiant group of about two dozen Lithuanians were standing on the wide, shallow steps of the fifteen-storey, dun-coloured tower block. There was grubby snow on the ground. A detachment of Soviet soldiers, in brown greatcoats and with bayonets fixed to their weapons, faced the protestors. The soldiers were squat, expressionless men from Central Asia, presumably chosen because they had as little as possible in common with the Baltic peoples. Their officer gave an order. The soldiers raised their guns and fired at the protestors. I was unable to believe that this was happening in front of me, and as it turned out I was right. As the cordite-scented smoke cleared, it became plain that the soldiers had been firing blanks. My father (having some experience of riot control during his pre-1939 years in the Royal Navy) had told me long before that this, like shooting over the heads of the crowd, is always a mistake. It makes the crowd think you are irresolute. So it proved. The Lithuanians, who to my intense admiration had not flinched in the face of apparent death, now came down the steps, filled with that fury that only fear can produce, and with fists and boots scornfully drove the soldiers back, bellowing insults at them in the Russian they had been carefully taught since kindergarten. The soldiers, astonishingly, took their punishment and retreated to a distance.

For the whole of that day there were repeated reports, some of them true, of other attempts by Moscow forces to seize control of key buildings. We chased from place to place all that bleak morning and freezing afternoon, following rumours and concluding that we were in an empire which had lost its mind. At last, worn out, we trailed to our hotel beds promising to wake each other if anything happened during the night.

And it did. As I faded into sleep, I was awakened by a great 'whump!', a giant, abnormal sound that obviously portended evil, and went to my hotel room window to see a warlike dark red glow on the horizon close to the Vilnius TV tower on a far edge of the capital. We all scrambled back into our trousers and set off to find out what wicked things were happening. I remember chasing a convoy of tanks down the highway in a taxi driven by a slightly unhinged driver (the knob on his gearstick was in the shape of a death's head, and luminous. The words 'Killer Commando' were inscribed in Gothic lettering on his windscreen), who tried to overtake the armoured column, until one of the tanks swung its gun barrel directly at our windscreen. All the journalists in the car were by this time yelling and shrieking at the driver to slow down, which he reluctantly did. But we still arrived at the TV tower in time to witness more shooting, which seemed – as most such things do – disorganised and random. Gunfire, even real gunfire, has a misleadingly jaunty sound, like a firework display, popping and crackling in a frivolous sort of way. In fact it was a straightforward attempt by Soviet special forces to take over TV broadcasting in the Republic, which failed only because whoever was ultimately in charge lost his nerve. I interviewed several defiant Lithuanians from a supine position in the muddy snow, urging them in vain to lie down as I was doing while the bullets pinged this way and that. 'What do you think of your wonderful Mr Gorbachev now?' I recall one of them asking me, quite reasonably peeved by the West's love affair with that ambiguous man, whose role in these events has never been properly explained. I did not think much of him, I confessed, as the dirty snow melted into the hair on the back of my head.

That night, Soviet soldiers murdered several people, whose bullet-mutilated bodies I would later see. The backs of their heads were in most cases missing in a rather disagreeable way that could not have been caused by a car crash. But the Soviet authorities had the nerve to claim, even months afterwards, that these corpses were the victims of 'traffic accidents'. The people of Vilnius responded to the gunnery by turning their Parliament building into a sort of mediaeval fortress. Every building site in the city was pillaged for concrete, and a colossal barricade was piled up on every approach road. In the entrance hall of the building itself, men in hastily invented uniforms stood guard with hosepipes connected to tanks full of petrol. They all recalled with bitter shame the failure of their grandfathers to fight Stalin when he had seized their country in 1939, and the terrible miseries of mass deportation that followed, worse than war. They also remembered that the Finns, a little later, had fought the Russian monster and saved their pride and much of their nation. Had the Soviets attacked again, there would have been screaming, blazing carnage. They did not attack again, which is why most readers of this book will not even know about those miserable days. The following evening we were invited by courageous Lithuanians to hide in their homes. They did not wish the only independent witnesses to a possible massacre to be rounded up and expelled. The morning afterwards, the Russians gave their feeble, lying press conference.

When it was over, I was very, very angry, in a consuming way that, for a while, made me treat every Russian I met with unfair spite and hostility. I returned to Moscow, sour and in a state of self-righteous rage against everything to do with Russia. I had previously been a little light-hearted about my assignment in the collapsing Utopia. After those nights in Vilnius, I realised properly just how dark a place I was in. Here, history was not safely contained in books, but reached out suddenly and poked you hard in the eye. I began to believe the worst things I heard about both the past and present, in a way I would never have done before.

Judging by his behaviour at that press conference, Jonathan Steele was, if anything, more enraged than I was –

I think this was because he felt he had been let down by his friends, the Gorbachev reform faction. Many in the Western Left had hoped that this time, the USSR could be turned into an exemplary state, which they would no longer need to be ashamed of. Gorbachev's failure was for them the final failure of the last, best hope for their secular religion.

I had no such illusions. I was a former Trotskyist who had never defended the Politburo. But it is more fiddly than that. I had been, from 1968 to 1975, a member of the International Socialists (IS), regarded by proper Trotskyists as heretics. The IS refused to acknowledge that the USSR was socialist at all, classifying it as 'State Capitalist'. In the theology of Trotskyism this was a serious sin, since it was more proper to regard the Soviet Union as a 'deformed' or 'degenerated' workers' state, and to believe that it should – in the last resort – be defended against capitalist attack. This led to all kinds of nonsense about the Soviet nuclear weapon, which we countered with a song called 'The Workers' Bomb' (to the tune of the 'Red Flag'). This concluded in mockery: 'Degenerated though it be, it's still the people's property/and, though our comrades all shout "Balls!", we'll stand beneath it when it falls.'

The others were more honest than we were. Ours was the extreme version of pretending that the USSR was not the fault of socialists, or even of Bolsheviks (which we wished to be). Of course it was their fault, the fault of people exactly like us, but we closed our minds to this with a web of excuses. We pretended not to be what we were, and that the USSR was not what it was. Yet where it was easy to do so we supported causes – the NLF in Vietnam in particular – whose objects were to extend Soviet power. What was vital – and remains vital now for serious revolutionary idealists – is that Communists *in power* must be classified as 'Stalinists', a special type of Marxist with which the modern revolutionary has nothing whatever to do. In this way, the revolutionary of today may always pretend that he will not be the tyrant of tomorrow. It is not true, but we convinced ourselves that it was.

The various warnings against tyranny by the German Spartacist Rosa Luxemburg and by Trotsky himself are often cited in support of this excuse-making view. There are many difficulties with this. Luxemburg, a defenceless woman, murdered by Freikorps louts, never lived to touch power and instead became a holy martyr of the Left. What if she had lived and become powerful? She would hardly be the first revolutionary to descend the broad, shallow staircase that leads from liberty to tyranny in the name of preserving the revolution from its enemies within and without. Nor are revolutionary women generally much gentler than their male counterparts. The wives of Erich Honecker and Nicolae Ceauşescu were both widely hated, in their own right, by the subjects of their husbands. Alexandra Kollontai was a menace, Nadezhda Krupskaya another – and there have been many thousands of Madame Defarges in the revolutions of the world. Luxemburg's party later distinguished itself by a stupid sectarianism which helped Hitler to power, combined with a dangerous intolerance of internal dissent. It is all very well for Marxist world-reformers to dislike the face of dictatorship once it is in power. Yet it is they who have summoned up this implacable figure, by their revolutionary incantations. Once summoned, he does not tend to go away again until he has killed by the thousands, or even millions.

What I saw in Poland, East Germany, Czechoslovakia and the USSR would help me to grasp this. But by the time I began to voyage beyond the Iron Curtain, I was already well prepared for a full apostasy.

Idealism and dogma are easier to sustain in a modern university campus than anywhere else on earth. There, you are free from the influences of home, subsidised into a fake independence which you think you have earned, spared the need to earn your bread, spared contact with the true drama of provincial life, and surrounded by arrogant and self-righteous people in their late teens, much like yourself – who think that they have discovered sex and idealism for the first time in the history of the human race.

This was not so easy in Swindon, the decayed railway town in which I served my apprenticeship as a newspaper reporter. I started my indentures on the *Evening Advertiser* intending to use my new skills in the service of the revolution, and I kept up a furtive contact with what we melodramatically called 'The Centre', our small but expensively equipped headquarters in an alley in Shoreditch. From time to time they would send me the details of someone who had filled in the enquiry slip published each week in our newspaper, the *Socialist Worker*. I would then call on them, like a sort of insurance salesman. One or two were reasonable, though the more reasonable they were, the less interested they were in getting involved and the more anxious they were to get me out of the house. Most were distressingly odd in one way or another, fulfilling Arthur Koestler's theory, expressed in his book *Arrival and Departure* that people who want to reform the world are generally in need of reform themselves. If it was true in these exaggerated cases, surely it was also true of me? One of these misfits lived in a village some way out of town, but on a wet and blustery evening I dutifully bicycled through the darkness to visit him and his cowering wife, who was obviously in fear of this rangy, hairy, muscular person. He seemed to be very revolutionary indeed, almost trembling with the desire to overthrow the existing order. But there was also something physically fearsome about him, not revolutionary at all.

A few days later, I was visiting other comrades in another town, which, having a university, attracted a rather more familiar class of Trotskyist. I mentioned this meeting to them. They exchanged haggard glances. 'Oh, so that's where ********* fetched up, is it?' inquired one.

'You know him, then?' I asked. The hairy man had never mentioned any connection with the university town to me.

'Yes, he's rather alarming, don't you find? He has a gun. We had to take it away from him during the Royal visit,' said the comrade, who was by no means a monarchist but could still see the risks to the movement if one of its members assassinated the Queen. I was too disturbed by the information to ask exactly how they had managed to disarm him, weedy pseudo-intellectual Marxists against a lithe, hot-eyed man in his prime, a man who possessed a firearm. But I felt that sensation, which was to be increasingly familiar, that a great dark hole, with no bottom, was opening up in the ground under my feet. I had spent the evening earnestly discussing the miners' case for more pay with an armed and dangerous lunatic. Once outside the warm, subsidised circle of the universities, this was the sort of mind that was attracted by our righteous creed. Not only did I never go to see him again, I ignored all the other slips that 'The Centre' passed on to me, and took to quietly dumping the small bundle of copies of the *Socialist Worker* which continued to arrive each Thursday night. I had to pay for them, of course, but it was worth it to avoid having to deliver them to the tiny group of unappealing people who would be my comrades if I wanted to carry on with the revolutionary cause.

By this time my reporter's job was bringing me into regular touch with the sort of people a student can ignore – policemen, court clerks, lawyers, firemen, Tory councillors, clergymen. And it also compelled me to see the world more or less as they did. When I wrote accounts of meetings, weddings, trials, fires and thefts, it was for them I was writing. After about two years of this, I could no longer square the world I had come to know with my fantasies of revolution. Unlike every other former revolutionary whose memoirs I have ever read, I do not claim to have 'just drifted away'. I actually did write a letter of resignation from the International Socialists, some time in early 1975. I did not keep a copy. But I hope they did, and that it was intercepted and filed by the Security Service.

7

A Fire Burning Under Water

By the late summer of 1980 I was a member of a strange and disreputable gang, the Fleet Street Industrial Correspondents. We were in truth a monstrous clique of Calibans, noisy, often drunk, inelegantly clad and profane. We regarded ourselves as a sort of elite corps of journalists, stealing glamour and excitement from the desperate, unhappy events we recorded. We were the people who wrote about the strikes that then constantly convulsed the country, helping to ruin what was left of its productive industry.

Most of us were socialists of one kind or another. I can only think of two or three exceptions among perhaps fifty people. Several were communist sympathisers or fellow-travellers. Others adopted such views so as to fit in better. Because the people we dealt with came for the most part from old heavy industries, with heavy-drinking traditions, they drank a great deal more than was good for them – and so did most of us. I would have done too, but alcohol makes me so ill that I couldn't (I mention this to make it clear that I don't claim any moral superiority over my more sodden colleagues). We were very busy for several years. There were many late nights leaning against walls outside pay talks, long weeks at union conferences in sad seaside towns, early morning stake-outs of mass meetings, late-night phone calls from the office as we were forced to follow the scoops of our rivals.

We generally quite liked our union contacts. Most of them had become officials because they were outstanding in some way – some cunning, some eloquent, some plain bloody-minded. They were very British. One of my favourites, an engineer, had been in the first wave on the beach at Arromanches on D-Day. But I had already developed a resistance to standard-issue Leftism, and I worked for a conservative newspaper, so to some extent I stood out against the general line of our gang, if partly for self-interested career reasons. I sought contacts among the unions which had resisted Left-wing takeovers. I favoured secret ballots and thought many strikes were plain wrong. I objected to the huge indirect influence which the tiny Communist Party exercised on the Labour Party, through its control of several unions and their block votes. To this day few people grasp just how important this was. I objected when my colleagues decided to affiliate the Industrial Correspondents' group (which was supposed to organise briefings and serve our collective interests) to a contentious body called 'the Campaign for Press Freedom'. My punishment for these eccentricities was to be called 'bonkers' – I have always seen this intentionally damaging sneer as an ultra-mild version of the Soviet state's classification of dissenters as mentally ill.

What follows is an example of my 'bonkers' behaviour. In the summer of 1980 the workers of the Lenin shipyard in Gdansk had astonished the world by challenging their Communist government. Amazingly unafraid of a malign and violent state, they had occupied the yard and demanded several freedoms which a Communist state could not possibly give them.

By September, they were grappling for their liberty – and possibly their lives – against the Polish Communist Party (technically known as the 'Polish United Workers' Party', a name so mendacious that it was funny). Nobody knew then that the Gdansk strikers would win in the end. The violent extinction of liberty in Prague had taken place only twelve years before. The British Trades Union Congress (TUC), then a far mightier institution than it is now, gathered for its conference in Brighton. The Polish shipyard strike was the most pressing issue before it. Here were workers, Trade Unionists, in a foreign country, peacefully facing an almighty employer with nothing but fraternity and the strike weapon. Surely the TUC would support these brothers?

Had they been workers in Chile, or South Africa, that support would indeed have come about. But they were striking against a socialist government, and so they were the wrong kind of brothers. Worse, from the TUC platform's point of view, they appeared to be at least partly motivated by patriotism and religion. What struck me than and still strikes me now is the shameless way in which the TUC leadership slithered away from giving the Gdansk workers the support they plainly needed and deserved. If anyone doubts that the British Labour Party was (and is) permeated with secret sympathy for Soviet Communism, this was the proof. Most of these men were – formally – democratic socialists and members of the Labour Party. But when it came to a choice, they instinctively took – despite much public derision – the side of a Communist despotism against their own apparent allies.

Having watched this disgrace (there were a couple of notable exceptions, the Electricians' leader Frank Chapple and the Engineers' leader Terry Duffy), I went to my then editor, a sensible and kindly man called Arthur Firth, too good for Fleet Street. I said to him 'I know I'm just the number two industrial reporter, but it seems to me that the most important strike anywhere in the world just now is happening in Gdansk. Will you send me there?' He thought for less than a minute before giving me his blessing. The visas took some weeks, and by the time my train crossed the River Oder from East Germany into Poland (passing a large group of Soviet soldiers camped next to the frontier), many feared a Russian invasion of Poland was imminent. The Western Alliance was not at its strongest. Ronald Reagan had just won the American presidential election, but would not succeed a weak and demoralised Jimmy Carter for two months.

In Poland, there was a strong feeling of a society at the end of its tether. Warsaw – which mostly lacked the beauty of Prague, and seemed far closer to Moscow in spirit, climate and architecture – was miserably cold and food was short even in hard-currency hotels. I flew in a juddering Russian plane to Gdansk (the single stewardess, for some reason, wore a riding helmet throughout the flight) and found the leader of the shipyard strike, Lech Wałęsa, in the flophouse hotel which was his headquarters. What did he think of the British TUC? I was used to British interviewees weighing their words. But not Wałęsa. I could hardly stop him. He despised them as cowards and toadies and said so in detail in every imaginable way. It was obvious that he should do so. Yet he was, far more than anyone I had ever met in England, comparable with the Tolpuddle Martyrs and the early fighters for the right to strike, with the Hunger Marchers and the indisputable heroes of the Labour movement with which I still had sympathy. And the nice, social democratic British Trades Union movement, who pretended to revere the men of Tolpuddle and Jarrow, when they were safely in the past, loathed such courage when they really met it in the present day. They were embarrassed by Wałęsa and Solidarity. They preferred to deal with the Polish official 'unions', wretched state-controlled organs infested with secret policemen.

That icy, foggy morning in the Hotel Morski, two streams of experience finally met in one place. It meant I could no longer be a socialist of any kind, though it would take me a few more years to admit it completely to myself. I described the things I saw and heard in Gdansk, men behaving as if they were free when they were not, as being like a fire burning under water. It was impossible in theory, yet visibly happening before my eyes. I was sure it could not go on for long. The same phrase could also have described my continuing attempts to reconcile my political faith with what I knew to be true. I would continue to hope that I was a socialist for several years, but the beams, joists and girders which held up my faith had all began to shift and tremble.

One other memory lingers very powerfully, from a little earlier, probably the 1978–9 'Winter of Discontent'. There was a pay dispute involving ambulance drivers. I had been promised by union officials I knew well that these drivers would do nothing which would delay or disrupt the emergency ambulance service. The persistent picture in my head is of an overwhelmingly grey, unfriendly bleak late winter afternoon on the wide Finchley Road in North London, with cars and lorries growling impatiently northward. There is a gritty wind. I am coming out of the Tube station (it must be my day off, for otherwise I would not be here at this hour) and I see and hear an accident about ten yards away. A car hits a woman who is trying to dodge through four lines of traffic. The bumper strikes her leg, not very fast, but fast enough to break the bone. There is an actual crunch, a sound so unusual that it can be heard above the general swish and snarl of vehicles. She cries out and falls, the traffic clots and stops, horns begin to blow, other pedestrians run towards her. Squeamish and medically useless, I dash back into the station to the bank of payphones there (this is long before the invention of mobiles) and call 999. Which service do I require? Ambulance, please. 'Sorry, there's an industrial dispute, ambulances are severely delayed … it could be at least an hour before someone can get to you.'

Now, about ten years before this I had crashed my motorbike and badly injured my leg, and had had to lie in some pain on the roadside waiting for an ambulance and occasionally glancing at the disagreeable mess I had made of my ankle and foot. I recalled how long it had seemed to take but I also recalled how much it had mattered to me to know that it was coming as fast as it could. I simply could not bring myself to go and tell the woman, now dragged to the roadside by passers-by and silent with shock and suffering, that she must wait at least an hour for mercy. Enraged by the exposed, blithe lies of the union men, whom I never trusted again on such matters, I stormed round to the surgery of my own excellent GP, who was just locking up to leave, and asked him to attend to the injured woman. So much for the considerate ambulancemen.

Like most industrial correspondents, I had identified with the people I wrote about and spent much of my time with, often making excuses for the strident conservatism of the paper I worked for, and dishonourably trying, through hints and gestures, to suggest that I dissented from its views. Not any more. From having been, more or less, on the side of the unions, I realised that the supposed prejudices of my own newspaper and others against the callousness of strikers were in fact far wiser than my own naive and simple-minded acceptance of a worthless assurance. By the time I met Lech Wałęsa in Gdansk, perhaps two years later, this triumph of experience over politics had gone deep into my mind. However much I wanted to stay in a political place that seemed safe and comfortable, I was no longer able to do so without consciously suppressing what I now knew to be true.

This made the Thatcher years complicated. I never liked her, though I was exhilarated and impressed by the way she was not taken in by anything about the USSR – so unlike most Tories. I also came to think that she was mostly right about the unions. But I couldn't identify with the car-obsessed, pinstriped, market-worshipping, greedy supporters she attracted. I particularly disliked the former Communist Alfred Sherman and his spiteful desire to concrete over railway lines. I saw him as a warning of what might happen to any ex-revolutionist if he did not know where to stop. Against the Labour Party, which I knew to be penetrated by all manner of Marxists, and soaked in the ideas of revolutionaries, it was increasingly necessary to support the Tories. This was partly because of the strikers' lies, but much more because of Poland and Czechoslovakia. On the Cold War, I knew she was right and the Left were wrong. I found my teenage belief in nuclear disarmament the most embarrassing of all, and made it my personal business to confront the silly revived Campaign for

Nuclear Disarmament (CND), attending their showings of Peter Watkins's propaganda film *The War Game* and pointing out that the horrors portrayed in it were the result of Soviet nuclear bombs – a fact that did not seem to have crossed their minds.

While I was still pondering these things, I began to spend more and more time in Eastern Europe, until I found myself living in Moscow, watching the end of the story I had seen beginning in Gdansk. I made one excursion home, asked by my then editor to harass Neil Kinnock in the 1992 general election (with some success). Then I moved to Washington. By the time I first encountered New Labour in 1995, I had been absent from British politics for almost five years.

There were several things I could not quite understand. One of them was political correctness. Another was the Labour Party's vehement loathing of good state education. Another was that the supposed Right wing in British politics did not seem to have any fight left in it, and was not conservative.

But the most puzzling and disturbing of all was the way that I repeatedly encountered changes in my own country which seemed to remind me of somewhere – some surliness or inefficiency, some invincible bureaucratic stupidity, some hatred or distortion of the past, but also a pervasive, leaden hostility to private life in the form of married parents raising their own children as they wished. And then it came to me that I was being reminded of the Soviet system under which I had lived in Moscow. Far from being defeated in the Cold War, social and cultural radicalism and the worship of power had escaped through the holes in the Berlin Wall, and begun to establish themselves in a morally and politically disarmed Britain.

I set out to try to solve these puzzles.

Part III

Britain through the Looking Glass

A Free People Freely Extinguish Their Own Freedom

8

Racism, Sexism and Homophobia: The Unholy and Divided Trinity

Racialism or racism?

Once upon a time I took part in a rather disgraceful demonstration against Enoch Powell. I still don't regret chanting anti-Powell slogans. I still regard his 1968 River Tiber speech as a piece of unscrupulous careerist stupidity and I am quite sure that it led directly to the ill-treatment of many of my fellow-creatures. But I am ashamed that our aim was to try to silence him, and I regret that I led a charge of fellow-teenagers against a police line outside Oxford Town Hall. Even so, it was a useful experience. We broke through the astonished old-fashioned coppers, scattering them with the force of our charge. And at that point, with the street empty before me I realised that *I had not the slightest idea of what to do next.* The protest was its own reward. I did not really want to burst into the hall and seize Mr Powell by his natty lapels. So we all melted back into the crowd before we could be arrested.

But I was protesting against something I still oppose – racialism, as we called it. I was completely persuaded that racial discrimination was unreasoning, wrong and inexcusable. I still am. I had a number of other views which I regarded as quite advanced at the time, about homosexuality and the place of women in society. Again, I still hold most of them, though I have discarded some and altered others now that I know a little more than I did then. Yet at some point in the years between then and now I discovered that quite a lot of people regarded me as what they called a 'racist', a 'sexist' and a 'homophobe'. Nothing I said or did seemed likely to alter this view. I was perplexed. How had I, the revolutionary rioter of forty years before, his head crammed with every 'progressive' opinion available, become these things?

The modern ideology of race is wholly different from our simple objection, in the 1960s and early 1970s, to what we then called 'racialism'. When I went on marches against Enoch Powell, or to support the admission to this country of the East African Asians, the issue was perfectly simple. People should not be treated differently because of the colour of their skin. Such discrimination was self-evidently unjust. It was also idiotic and wasteful of talent and hope. A man's colour said nothing important about him. What mattered, as Martin Luther King had (then quite recently) said was 'the content of his character'. The whole point of King's biblically phrased and now too rarely read speech was that black and white would and could grow up as equal citizens judged only by their actions. Justice would flow down like waters and right- eousness like a mighty stream. It was, to my generation, a mark of stupidity to think otherwise. I knew racial discrim- ination was wrong not just because it disgusted my instincts, but because it was irrational. It was wasteful of talent and friendship and based upon the crudest and most easily disproved prejudice. It was a denial of hope.

I still remember, while under arrest one August night in 1969, being amazed to see in a London police station a printed, laminated official notice detailing the different proce- dures to be used when charging 'men of colour'. I wish I had had the foresight to memorise it, since I am sure all copies have long ago been thrown down the memory hole. I suspect it would be disturbingly similar – in its basic logic – to some of the rules in operation since the avowedly racialist (and anti- racist) Macpherson report into the Stephen Lawrence affair, which specifically called for an end to 'colour-blind policing' and recommended special treatment for ethnic minorities. This is the most fundamental revolution in thought in the last thirty years, the almost imperceptible slither away from the simple loathing of bigotry, which we in the 1960s and early 1970s pursued, and towards a revolutionary attempt to adapt society into a multicultural shape. Yet it is treated as if it is a continuous development of the anti-racialist campaigns of forty years ago, when it is plainly not.

One of the most important steps in this process was the dropping of the word 'racialist', which I accept was difficult to shout, write on placards or paint on walls, and the adoption of the word 'racist'. Even so, it is interesting that it is sometimes written, or scrawled 'RASCIST', a spelling error which is also an ideological elision. The word 'Fascist' was long ago dismissed as an empty insult by George Orwell, in his 1946 essay 'Politics and the English Language'. He said: 'The word *Fascism* has now no meaning except in so far as it signifies "something not desirable".' And yet it is still in daily use by people who prefer emotion to reason. I think there is modern evidence of this in the strange coinage 'Islamo-fascism', and the fashionable description of Jihadist terrorists as 'fascist'. These expressions were used almost simultaneously, in August 2006, by the Republican evangelical Christian George W. Bush and the former Communist British Home Secretary John Reid. Both were referring to an alleged terror plot to explode aeroplanes above the Atlantic, a political method which has no historic connections with any violent, conservative authoritarian movement, but rather with those sometimes sympathised with by the Left, such as the Arab campaign against Israel.

Mr Reid is more intelligent than Mr Bush. He also comes from a wholly different political tradition in which the word 'fascist' does heavy duty because 'National Socialist' is ideologically troubling, as it contains the awkward word 'socialist'. The word 'Nazi' is also difficult for Communists as it reminds people of the Molotov–Ribbentrop or Nazi–Soviet Pact. By contrast, President Bush's knowledge of European politics between the two world wars is likely to be scanty, and I would doubt if he could distinguish a fascist from a Nazi, or come up with the Christian names of either Molotov or Ribbentrop.

It is not possible that both men could have meant the same thing when they used this word, even though they were using it about the same people on the same day. Orwell's conclusion, that it means nothing more than 'I think this is bad' is beautifully borne out. His implied message, that we should mistrust those who use it because they are bound to be trying to manipulate us, is also confirmed. I think much the same could now be said about 'Racist' and 'Racism'. I should be interested if anyone could trace the change from 'racialist' to 'racist' in mainstream usage in Britain. It was probably first imported from the USA during the Black Panther era. But why did the new expression so completely supplant the older word? I suspect that it was accompanied by a profound change in meaning which probably came from the same North American source and had its roots in Black Separatism and the other disturbing ideas which came to obsess such figures as Stokely Carmichael, and have been carried even further by Louis Farrakhan. Interestingly, these are people who might well be accused of 'racialism', especially in their publicly expressed attitudes towards Jews and their strange tendency to admire Hitler.

A 'racialist' could only be a person who believed in unalterable racial differences, and in the superiority of some racial groups over others. This was the word's precise meaning, usually dated back to the prescriptive racial theories of Houston Stewart Chamberlain, who was (conveniently for the links we liked to make in the late 1960s) a Nazi sympathiser who actually took German citizenship and maintained that Jesus Christ was an Aryan. I think it was this precision, and this history, which led to the word being abandoned. It was too exact for its new and very different use. The newer term, on the other hand, was vague enough to suggest all kinds of things without actually needing to make specific, deniable accusations. In my (quite considerable) experience of being politically defamed, a person does not need to express or even privately feel any racial prejudice to be called a 'racist'. He does not need to embrace any theory of racial superiority or unalterable difference. Nor does he need to engage in acts of wrongful discrimination based on race or colour. If an organisation is being accused, then the charge of 'institutional racism' widens the mouth of the net, and narrows its gauge, still further. One of the most fascinating facts of our time is this: that the (widely unread) Macpherson report into the Lawrence affair found not one single instance of actual racial discrimination in the Metropolitan Police handling of the case, and so found it easier to convict that force of 'institutional racism', a charge so vague that there is no effective defence against it.

This misleading name-calling and its effect on public policy is a large problem for our society. But let us return to the use of 'racist' to describe a person. A helpful (to the zealot) confusion is created by the fact that all racialists are racists (just as all Jihadists are Muslims) but not all racists are racialists (just as not all Muslims are Jihadists). So the racist may truly be a racial bigot, a Holocaust denier and secret Nazi sympathiser, and may himself actively discriminate between people on irrational grounds. But he may do none of these things. He will, entirely unjustly, often find himself classified and dismissed as a racist if he is in fact what ought to be called a 'culturist', someone who believes that migrants should adapt to the country in which they arrive, rather than the other way round. This is how I would describe someone who uses expressions such as 'host country' (which I have heard angrily booed at a meeting in North Kensington held to discuss the Lawrence affair) and who states or implies that the existing culture of this country is worth preserving or indeed badly needs to be preserved.

The term 'racist' confuses the issue, allows for easy smears, guilt by association, and generally silences almost anyone who is accused of this, the worst thought-crime of our age. There is another problem here. Many, who in their lives and actions oppose and eschew all racial discrimination, do so because they have been successfully educated into better behaviour and better manners during the last thirty years. They may have collected golliwog badges as children and heard their parents using racial epithets in the privacy of home. They may retain private instincts or prejudices, which they suppress because they honestly believe them to be wrong, yet which are still racialist. Accused of 'racism', such people are often reluctant to defend themselves, since they fear an inquisition which will try to make windows into their very souls – and the very vagueness of the charge is a threat.

There is another more important way in which the charge of 'racism' is abused. Those who believe that culture, rather than race, is a defining characteristic of peoples are often smeared with the charge of 'racism'. Yet their position is the exact opposite of the argument of the bigots with whom they are being corralled. Why is racialism wrong, not just repulsive to the instincts and associated with ignorance and cruelty, but wrong as a matter of fact? It is wrong because it is not true. The worst thing about racialism is its hopelessness, the dismal assumption that there are unalterable barriers between peoples decided by birth and heredity. If this theory were true, then a thousand years of integration would mean nothing. Worse still, hostility between racial groups, if it existed in the first place, could never be expected to die. The culturist – and a good example of this view, plainly stated, is the American conservative thinker Thomas Sowell – believes something wholly different. He thinks that under the influence of history, economics, climate, religion, language, law, education, landscape, music and morals, people of any racial background can become one through the accumulation of a common cultural capital.

If this is so, then a powerful monoculture – learned by all – is an important weapon in the fight to achieve integration. It is, in fact, the only reliable strategy to defeat racialism. The alternative, of maintaining and encouraging many cultures in a society, is likely to frustrate integration and perpetuate division – especially if those many cultures are based on ethnic groups, as they generally are. In modern Britain this has actually happened. Yet the campaigners against racism have until recently been enthusiastic supporters of multicultur- alism, and have been only too willing – as I can witness – to condemn supporters of a monoculture as 'racist'. This position would not make sense if their main aim was to abolish racial division and hatred. It does make sense if they are understood as revolutionaries who ruthlessly use the weapon of smear and accusation against their critics – or as the dupes of such revolutionaries.

The point where this ridiculous falsehood reaches breaking strain is the point at which the Left chooses to defend Islam against its Western critics, on the ground that rejection of Islam, or a dislike of Islamic practices, is a branch of racism, sometimes called 'Islamophobia'. Yet a dislike of some Islamic beliefs is perfectly rational, and virtually compulsory among those who consider themselves enlightened on such subjects as female liberation, tolerance of homosexuals and opposition to racial prejudice.

The frequent and often seemingly racialist (and certainly racist) denunciations of Jews by Islamic preachers are surely utterly indefensible. Yet Muslim clerics who endorse hatred of Israel are welcomed and praised by leading figures of the multi- cultural Left. Such people would condemn such bigotry if it took any other form. Revolutionary groups such as the Socialist Workers' Party have also made shameful accommodations with Muslims. There is a general tendency on the Left to support Islamic causes – in Bosnia and in Israel. Radical feminists have even attempted to suggest that Islamic dress codes for women are in some way liberating. If examined thoughtfully, this confusion is ridiculous beyond belief. Yet a modern doublethink permits it to continue, sometimes unnoticed, often excused and not even properly laughed at. The supposedly enlightened liberal finds himself insisting that the shrouding of women in public frees them from the sexual contest and display imposed upon their Western sisters, and falling silent over forced marriages, the general legal subjection of women under Sharia law, the persecution of homosexuals, the swirling Judophobia and all the rest of the mediaeval baggage which arrives in the train of the Muslim faith.

There is worse than this. A horrible amalgamation has taken place between Islam's long dislike of Jews, expressed many times in the Koran and the Hadith, and modern Western Judophobia. This is best symbolised by Haj Amin al Husseini, Grand Mufti of Jerusalem between World War I and World War II, an unremitting foe of Zionism, who (finally rejected by his one-time British colonial sponsors) sought asylum in wartime Berlin. There he consorted with leading National Socialists, and helped to recruit a Muslim division of the SS (the Hanschar Division) in the Balkans. This sinister connection continued after the war, symbolised by the long-standing residence of the National Socialist child murderer Alois Brunner in the Syrian capital, Damascus. Syria is also well-known for the systematic persecution of its remaining Jews.

Discredited garbage, such as the 'Protocols of the Elders of Zion' originally forged by the Tsarist secret police, now circulate as if genuine in the Arab world, as do the sort of blood-libel myths once common in Europe (especially the supposed use of Christian children's blood to bake Jewish pastries).

This poison has spread throughout the Islamic world. During a visit to Burnley soon after racial and cultural disturbances there, I found Henry Ford's Judophobic volume *The International Jew* on display in an Islamic bookshop in the Daneshouse area, now largely inhabited by people who originate from Pakistan. Ford himself grudgingly withdrew this book from circulation, in his lifetime, but this was a recent edition with a cover illustration of a hook-nosed Jew that could have come straight from the National Socialist Jew-baiting newspaper *Der Stürmer*. It is surprising how many people have persuaded themselves that Islam is a 'religion of peace' when it has never claimed to be so, or that it is a 'religion of tolerance' when any historical study of Islamic rulers' treatment of Jews and Christians (especially the 'Pact of Umar') reveals that this alleged 'tolerance' makes Apartheid South Africa look like an egalitarian society.

I had better add here that – despite these and other reservations – I regard Muslims as allies against the current fashion for militant atheism, and against the moral chaos which it is creating. I have spent many happy hours debating and arguing with them. I have enjoyed their hospitality in several countries, and have been impressed by their cheerful willingness to argue with a Christian who denies many of their most treasured beliefs (we would get on with them better if we were not be so scared of disagreeing with them, and so lacking in confidence in our own beliefs). But I decline to pretend that their faith, taken seriously, is compatible with the sort of society I wish to live in. And I have told them so. The conventional Leftist, who views defenders of a monoculture as racists, finds himself drawn irresistibly into defending or apologising for Islam, since it is the foe of British monoculture, and is the religion of an important and politically significant ethnic group. He is less keen to observe that Islam is not itself an ethnic group. In fact he commends it for being non-racialist. He fails to observe, or prefers not to notice, that its hostility to Jews, though religious in origin, is necessarily racial in application. He excuses this as a manifestation of the 'anti-Zionism' which has (rather oddly) become one of the pillars of conventional Leftism in the past forty years. And until recently he has not realised just how hostile Islam is to the sexual and cultural revolution which he treasures above all. It is the discovery of Islam's genuine social conservatism, and its intransigent theism, which has caused a number of prominent Left-wingers to speak of 'Islamic fascism'. These critics were strangely unmoved for decades by the anti-Western, anti-Israeli terrorism of Fatah or Hamas, or the almost invariable lack of liberty in Islamic states.

You might have thought that a contradiction as obvious as the one between holding Leftist opinions and apologising for Islam would lead to the sort of mental conflict which produces a change of mind. But in many cases it does not. And even where it does, the change is often only partial. The enlightened Leftist is outraged to the point of incandescence by Muslim attacks on Manhattan, but equivocal about Muslim attacks on West Jerusalem or Tel Aviv, and silent about the Muslim persecution of Christians throughout the Arab world.

Doublethink, the strange ability to hold two contradictory opinions at the same time, steps in and saves the conventional liberal from a serious brainstorm. The interesting question is how and why that doublethink functions. My own view, from my own experience of reluctantly changing my mind, is that this is brought about – in the honest person – by a fear of what other revisions would follow a concession on this issue. The wall that stands between the Left-wing person and a loss of his or her faith is often thin enough to allow a blurred glimpse of what lies beyond.

This wall is strong precisely because it is so thin and transparent. In the mind of the honest person it is held in place by a perfectly reasonable fear of where revisionist thinking might lead. It is not breached, precisely because the conventional Leftist knows that a large and serious personal reformation, involving the loss of friends and possible career damage, lies on the other side of it. I suspect that the thing the Leftist fears most of all is surrender to the loathly opposite of humanist utopianism, the Christian religion. This, certainly for the member of the 1960s university generation, is the thing he has sought to escape, along with the suburban house, the dull office job and the quiet, undramatic marriage of his parents.

I believe people often understand far more about their opponents' ideas than they appear to, and know that what appear to be a few easy steps along a pleasant road of mild revision can end in a political and moral journey of thousands of miles. This is why they never take the first step, and why they fend off articulate criticism with anger, ostracism and abuse rather than with reason. This is why I abandoned the idea of writing a book entitled 'How to Change Your Mind'. It became clear to me that most people hate the very idea of changing their minds, while claiming to be open-minded. In the same way, most people hate freedom of speech, except for those who completely agree with them. But they pretend otherwise.

In the mind of the unscrupulous person the wall is kept in place by political convenience, by the need to build voting coalitions. This is less complicated and less interesting. I am more interested in the scrupulous people.

The formula of 'anti-racism' does not make sense on its own terms, is hostile to thought and debate, helps no oppressed person, and is not an organic continuation of the just and laudable campaigns for integration and equality which convulsed the Western world four decades ago. Yet the formula is not questioned precisely because it would be risky to question it. Those who doubt it face wrath instead of reason – anger with an opponent being an almost invariable sign of fear that he may be right.

Those who doubt the conventional view have been classified as the modern equivalent of heretics, contemptible people who must be condemned, not reasoned with. This is a pity, since much damage is being done by the Left's willingness to allow this lazy confusion to exist. The Left may be immovable, but the rest of society needs to escape from the false logic of 'anti-racism' if we are to construct a workable and fair policy on migration, to reach a wise accommodation with Islam, or to reconstruct a society whose solidarity has been terribly damaged by multiculturalism. Yet, for the reasons given above, I do not expect this to happen.

Where, in all this, are the ideals of the Left of forty years ago? Would those who demonstrated alongside me against Enoch Powell ever have imagined that their campaign would lead to incessant state registration of racial or ethnic characteristics? No. They would have regarded such lists with dislike and suspicion, associating them with racialist regimes such as the old South Africa or even National Socialist Germany. Would they even for a moment have thought that their comrades would seek to make peace with Islam, especially its Judophobia and its repression of women, for the sake of a political alliance? No. They would have regarded such an arrangement as immoral and unworkable.

The Left finds itself up to its knees in these paradoxes because – deprived of its old aims by the end of the Cold War and the end of heavy industry – it needs new masses to serve as a replacement proletariat. It too readily and thoughtlessly accepted Muslims as convenient substitutes for the white working class which has now ceased to support it, or vanished altogether. It has also fallen under the influence of revolutionaries far more subtle and effective than the Russian Bolsheviks or the Trotskyist rump. The gaping space left by the death of classical political revolutionary socialism has been filled by the spirit of 1968. That spirit will accept almost any ally against social and cultural conservatism, and against the Christianity that lies beneath those forces. This is why the sexual revolution has become so inseparably linked to the cultural and political revolutions.

The 1968 ideology is not merely a ready-made and self-righteous political system, with a clear position on every major controversy. It is a limitless process of personal liberation from conscience, guilt and restraint, dressed up in the flashy robes of moral superiority. These features are happily combined – in this particular generation – with personal ambition and worldly wealth. In all the most well-regarded and rewarded trades and professions, especially broadcasting, the law and the arts, a full set of 1968 opinions is an asset and an aid to advancement. Rejection of these opinions is a grave disadvantage.

One of the serious mistakes of George Orwell's *Nineteen Eight-Four* was the assumption that the revolutionary state would necessarily be sexually repressive (Julia wears the sash of the 'Junior Anti-Sex League' and Winston Smith's affair with her is one of his main acts of subversion). This has tended to be true only when such states were preparing for old-fashioned wars requiring enormous conscript armies and great numbers of babies. At all other times, there are very good reasons why such a state must be at war with private life, religion and the marriage-based morality that sustains them both. Even Stalin's Soviet Union, while it reacted against the early sexual liberation promoted in the 1920s by such campaigners as Alexandra Kollontai, ensured that divorce remained cheap and easy. It also attacked parental authority through the grotesque cult of Pavlik Morozov, the (probably mythical) child-martyr who denounced his own parents to the secret police and was killed by his grandfather. This cult was one of the most important features of Soviet life, yet remains largely unknown to Westerners who have only the vaguest idea of the extent and cruelty, rage and fury of the Soviet state's war against the married family and religion. Yet it foreshadows many of the laws and attitudes which increasingly limit the powers of Western parents to discipline or control their own children, and which will readily classify them as 'abusers' – presumed guilty by the legal system – if they try to do so.

Only foolish tyrants look to *Nineteen Eighty-Four* as a model for their societies and these – Ceauşescu's Romania and Kim il Sung's North Korea – can never fully co-opt their subjects and are in constant danger from the truth. Cleverer despots recognise that Aldous Huxley's *Brave New World*, in which power destroyed the family and harnessed pleasure to its purposes, was more likely to succeed and endure. Sexual licence, narcotic drugs and endless diverting entertainment, followed by swift and painless euthanasia when the faculties fail, dispense with the need for a thought police. There are few if any thoughts that need to be policed. In such societies, dissent is an eccentricity. Nobody need care about covering up the truth, since nobody is interested in it. Nobody need suppress the past, since nobody cares about it. And there is nothing necessarily revolutionary about sexual licence.

Slaves in history have often been allowed to copulate and reproduce, if only to breed more slaves, but seldom if ever permitted true marriage or family life.

So the sexual revolution is, by a great paradox, a revolution against political consciousness, discontent and rebellion. The sexual revolutionary climbs over the barricades and straight into bed with someone he is not married to, and quite possibly someone of the same sex. He is not seeking the overthrow of the existing order. He is seeking the existing order's permission to pursue pleasure at all costs. The idea that sex is necessarily connected with reproduction and parenthood is actually repulsive and shocking to him. He is also engaged in a war against continuity, a rejection of his parents' lives, and a rejection of guilt. And guilt, as Sigmund Freud did so much to show, can most easily be avoided by ensuring that actions previously viewed as guilty become normal and general.

This is why the sexual insurgent eventually finds himself ranged against all the outer defences of Christian civilisation – the canon of literature, classical music, representational art, traditional architecture, modest dress and seemliness of all kinds, restraint in speech, decorum and manners in general. All these embody or imply Christian mythology and Christian ideas about guilt, penitence, redemption and conscience. Conscience, allied with absolute morality and sustained by religion, is the source of guilt. This is why, sooner or later, the Western sexual radical is bound to attack Christianity, because it is his own religion and the basis of the guilt and self-restraint which he wishes to discard. He may simultaneously be happy to give sympathy to other religions, but this is because they are practised by migrants whom he sees as allies against the monoculture. It is also because he did not meet these faiths in his childhood or learn them from his parents, and so does not feel that they bind him as Christianity would, if he accepted it.

He may take some years to arrive at this direct anti-God position, since first he will have been busy smashing the outer fortifications of Christian sexual morality – disapproval of pre-marital and extra-marital sex, prohibitions on abortion and divorce, misgivings about homosexuality. But once these are out of the way the inner fastness of Christian belief lies exposed, and open to attack. The likely end of the culture wars will be an enraged smashing and desecration of the altars, a moment brilliantly prefigured in fiction in Simon Raven's 1970 novel *Places Where They Sing*, in which a Cambridge college chapel is obscenely profaned by a student mob – but also prefigured in fact in a disturbing incident in New York City in 1989, curiously like Raven's imaginary outrage. An organisation called ACT UP had launched a protest against the Roman Catholic Church, because of its views on contraception, abortion, homosexuality and sex education. On 10 December that year, supporters of ACT UP invaded St Patrick's Cathedral during High Mass, forcing Cardinal O'Connor to abandon his sermon. Demonstrators lay down in the cathedral aisles, 'chained themselves to pews, threw condoms in the air or shouted invective at the Cardinal. One former altar boy deliberately dropped a consecrated Communion wafer on the floor' (John-Manuel Andriote, *Victory Deferred*, University of Chicago Press, Chicago, 1999, p 247).

Many campaigners for sexual revolution correctly decided that this behaviour was a tactical mistake, being likely to lose sympathy rather than gain it, and it has not been repeated. But I suspect that it illustrates the real feelings of many sexual liberationists towards the Christian Church – feelings which cannot really be classified as tolerant or pluralist. If Christianity can be deprived of its position in Western societies, and made a purely private motto, the sexual revolutionary can be reasonably confident that the limits on his own choice, which he hates so much, will never return. Rather than staging violent invasions of churches, the opponents of religion have embarked on a long march through the places where Christianity was once supreme – schools, adoption agencies, charities – and quietly dethroned religion. They have – probably instinctively rather than intentionally –

dismantled the foundations of marriage (for the details of this legislative and cultural campaign, see my *Abolition of Britain*, Continuum, London, 2008). They have begun to raise the possibility of disestablishing the Church of England, and they have consistently misinterpreted the US Bill of Rights to attack religion in the public square in the USA. It is the spirit of 1968 that has been the great engine of this change, and the war against guilt and self-restraint that has been the engine of the 1968 movement.

It is not over yet. Once they have won, sexual liberationists who demand tolerance for themselves are unlikely to accord tolerance to their opponents. While they await that moment, they continue to fight as furiously and illogically about sex as they do about race.

9

Sexism is Rational

Of course the irrational oppression of women is wrong, as is every thought or action based upon the idea that women are inferior to men. The just person must reject any such ideas of unearned superiority of one human over another, which are the intellectual foundations of slavery. I cannot see how any civilised human being could believe anything different. There is not a word of Virginia Woolf's *A Room of One's Own* with which I could disagree, yet because I resist some other, wholly different, ideas, many of my opponents assume automatically that I believe in the subjection of women as domestic chattels. I am diagnosed with a pathology called 'Sexism', which (like 'Racism' and 'Homophobia') instantly diminishes me into a suffering, irrelevant and contaminated person, whose arguments do not need to be listened to, and who must first be crushed and then perhaps pitied.

Yet again, there is no logic in this. One thing is being confused with another that is quite distinct from it. This alliance between political Leftism and revolutionary or radical feminism embodies the Left's decisive change from nineteenth-century social democracy, aimed at the capture of state power and the economy, to twentieth-century moral, cultural and sexual radicalism, aimed at the through-and-through trans-formation of social relations, and at a complete moral revolution. As it happens, the Marxist Left of the 1960s and early 1970s were not especially feminist. I seem to remember a fair amount of crude and backward attitudes being expressed towards women by many of my male comrades in that era. If the personal is political then the comrades were about as male-chauvinist as the clientele of White's Club.

The revolution did not express much interest in this subject until some years after that. I do not, for example, remember anyone feeling particularly uncomfortable about the lyrics of such Rolling Stones songs as 'Under my Thumb' (see below) or 'Look at that Stupid Girl'. A sample from this masterpiece follows:

> She's the worst thing in this world
> Well, look at that stupid girl
> Shut-up, shut-up, shut-up, shut-up, shut-up
> Shut-up, shut-up, shut-up, shut-up, shut-up
> Shut-up, shut-up, shut-up

But during this period the lyrics of popular songs often contained strong cultural or political messages ('Sympathy for the Devil', 'Street Fighting Man', 'Revolution', 'You've Got to Admit it's Getting Better', 'Let's Spend the Night Together' (whose lyrics were changed in the more puritan USA to 'Let's Spend Some Time Together'), 'She's Leaving Home', 'When the Ship Comes in', 'The Times They Are A-Changing', 'Blowing in the Wind' and many others). And in those days the Rolling Stones were considered (and considered themselves) just as much part of the general radical movement (see my account of the Mick Jagger and Keith Richards trials in my book *The Abolition of Liberty*) as the Vietnam solidarity campaigners or the nuclear disarmers.

Their song lyrics had more influence than any amount of Herbert Marcuse's prose. In fact, during the fascinating and forgotten few weeks in 1967 when Mr Jagger and Mr Richards were prosecuted on drugs charges, their rivals, The Who, specifically chose to record a version of 'Under my Thumb' as a tribute and a gesture of support. I seem to remember that it began and ended with the sound of cell doors slamming, to remind us all of the appalling martyrdom of Mick and Keith. Why would they have picked this particular song unless it was seen as typical of them and good in itself? The song, for those too young to recall its words, could nowadays be sung without much difficulty by a Taleban rock band, with a backing group of women in burqas. 'It's down to me. The way she does just what she's told ... Under my thumb, her eyes are just kept to herself, under my thumb, well I, I can still look at someone else.'

The strand of feminism which demands education, the vote, property rights and legal equality between spouses does not come into serious conflict with social and moral conservatism. Why should it? An educated woman does not have to cash her education in to work for a corporation, though she is free to do so. She is not wasted as a mother of children – on the contrary, she is likely to be a far better mother than an uneducated woman – and raising the next generation is one of the most responsible and essential tasks in any society, one of the best uses of education imaginable. Such changes strengthen institutions and allow traditions to survive. In this case it is stupidity and fear among conservatives which are to blame for inconsistency, injustice and waste. One main reason for the continuing false division in the great discussions dividing society is official conservatism's refusal to abandon genuinely discredited positions.

What can they have been thinking of when they opposed the legal equality of the sexes, or tried to stop women studying at Oxford or Cambridge? Their folly handed a sharp and lethal weapon to the ultra-feminists. That weapon is this argument: 'They opposed the vote for women. They opposed university education for women. They opposed the admission of women to the professions. They were wrong. Now they oppose absolute equality in the workplace, and the replacement of marriage by other arrangements. They must be wrong about that too, *and for the same reason*.' And yet the arguments are wholly different. But until the wise conservative thoroughly and apologetically concedes the earlier mistakes, and also breaks decisively from all sorts of racial bigotry, he cannot possibly resist the demands of the new ultra-feminist cause or of multiculturalism. One of the major problems with conservatism is that it has seldom been willing to concede that the Left was right about any of these things.

This is partly because political conservatism has almost always disliked thought. It has tended to concede victory to the Left not because it was actually persuaded by the Left's arguments, but because it was too weak to oppose them any more. If it is to survive at all, it will have to learn to change this habit. The current alignment of 'Left' and 'Right' does not encourage this. It leaves many social conservatives trapped in factions which continue to articulate thoughtless prejudices. It allows the Left to pretend that it alone supports the liberation of women. This is far from true.

The new feminism which emerged from the USA in the 1970s did not want rational equality of two different sexes, but wanted women treated exactly as if they were men. Because women are very different from men, the effect of this was bound to be unfair to one sex or the other. In general, it has been unfair to men, though it has had some bad unintended consequences for women – especially by making employers more reluctant to hire them, and men less willing to marry them. It directly challenged marriage and it severely devalued work inside the home. It made a fetish of paid work outside the home as being the field in which equality must be achieved. It insisted that women should be permitted to do almost everything that men did – from flying US Navy jets to crewing British fire engines. But these were deliberate assaults on totems of maleness, which often led to misery and disappointment for the women who found themselves being thrust on to the barricades. The tragic death of the US Navy F-14 pilot Kara Hultgreen, under immense pressure to succeed on behalf of her sex, is a particularly poignant example of this. There has never been much of a campaign for women to invade such unglamorous all-male fields as the collection and emptying of dustbins. The demand for equality even where it defied logic was as different from its predecessors as anti-racist multiculturalism is from the original civil rights movement.

The older feminism was what revolutionary Marxists describe as a 'reformist' movement, aimed at improving conditions within the existing order. The new feminism is a revolutionary movement, intended to overthrow that order and replace it with a new world. The original 1960s revolutionaries had little time for this part of the struggle, at least at first. They were possessed by the idea that the working class would make the revolution. These were the days when Britain still had great armies of male industrial workers organised into Trades Unions and astonishingly willing to go on strike. These were the times of combat between Edward Heath and whichever group of manual workers he happened to be fighting that week. And even we Trotskyists made some connections with these disgruntled manual workers. Oxford International Socialists recruited at least one highly effective Trade Unionist in the Pressed Steel works, as well as a cheerful if often baffled group of dustmen who liked our spirit. In York, there were several bus drivers and conductors, a shop steward from a glassworks and a scattering of individuals from the city's chocolate factories. I personally nursed a small Bolshevik cell in a coachbuilding works in Scarborough, often being ferried to meetings by the sea (and given lavish meals on the way) by the great and much-lamented historian, Gwyn Williams. Professor Williams did not actually agree with our detailed policies, but thought we deserved support anyway, for our revolutionary élan.

We became so apparently successful that we were also targeted by the security service – at least I have always assumed this explained the appearance among us of various self-proclaimed ex-policemen or ex-servicemen, allegedly mature students, supposedly disaffected and hostile to their former masters, amazingly willing to sell the *Socialist Worker* at Goole Docks at five o'clock in the morning. Such people tended to be pretty socially conservative, though some of them rather enjoyed the admiration of the more attractive female comrades, who were thrilled to be in the company of real workers instead of weedy students, and to be fighting for the cause as well. The world of body-fascism, speculums, female separatism and political lesbianism, abortion as a positive act, and the rest of the ultra-feminist agenda were an isolated strand of Left-wing politics in Britain until the 1980s. Anti-marriage, anti-motherhood, anti-husband feminism's sudden growth and expansion, and its amazingly swift acceptance by the mainstream of publishing and commerce surely had much more to do with the changed demands of modern business than with any intellectual triumph.

For by this time, capitalism did not want men any more, at least not as many of them and not for the same sorts of jobs. They were hard to handle, trained for industries that had ceased to exist, and formed powerful Trades Unions. Their work was better done in China, India or Korea, for much lower wages. It wanted women, who tended to give their loyalty more fully, were more diligent, better-suited to the less physical work increasingly on offer, more reliable and hard-working, and were also bad at collective action. This was wholly rational sex discrimination, dressed up as the abolition of sex discrimination. One minute the idea that all women should go out to work as a matter of principle was confined to the readers of *Spare Rib* and its collective. The next moment *Spare Rib* had died from lack of support, but its views had been almost wholly embraced by *Cosmopolitan* and the agony aunts of otherwise conservative Fleet Street newspapers, whose rapid switch away from endorsing marital propriety and full-time motherhood was one of the most astonishing turnabouts since the Molotov–Ribbentrop Pact.

I do not think enough attention has been paid to the incredible swiftness and ease of this conquest. Would genuine revolutionaries really have wanted Helen Gurley Brown, author of *Sex and the Single Girl*, advancing their honoured banners on the field of conflict? Whether they did or not, that is what they got, ending up with the noble pleas of Mary Wollstonecraft reduced to the grunts and squeals of 'Girl Power' and the raucous equality-in-grossness of the hard-drinking and lewd 'Ladette'. It is hard to see who has benefited from it apart from major employers, abortion clinics, alcohol manfacturers and the state. It is the state which in the crudest sense gets the extra taxes, and in a deeper victory sees its old adversary, the married family, weakened to the point where it now barely exists. The decline in marriage has been one of the swiftest and least noted social changes in British history, as has the disappearance of the full-time mother and the appearance of a gigantic network of day-orphanages for the children left motherless for five days of each week as a result. It is plain that children have suffered badly as a result of it, though being powerless and having no idea that there was any alternative, they have never protested. It is also clear that private life, that essential shelter for free thought and free speech, has been much reduced by it.

Under this new bargain, business exploits women on a scale not seen since Victorian times. Government and commerce have also forced their way much more deeply into private life. Yet this change, ambiguous at best, is identified as an unmixed humanitarian or beneficial cause by social radicals who would be against it, as crude exploitation, if it took almost any other form.

What is truly liberating (or socialist, or even radical) about swapping home life, with its independence and personal freedom, for wage slavery and the tax slavery that invariably comes with it? What is Left-wing about the vast, greedy industry of baby farms, in which the young are minded by legions of paid strangers with no long-term interest in their charges? Wage-slave women are a cruelly exploited new class, as an old-fashioned nineteenth-century radical would instantly see. But the modern left is a vociferous supporter of the exploiters. It is left to the tougher religions, and to despised social conservatives, to oppose it.

As with the transformation of anti-racialism into the wholly different 'anti-racism', a campaign to liberate women from domestic oppression has changed into a wholly different and effectively opposite campaign to enslave women in offices and call centres. There they are actually oppressed by managers who can sack them, and who have no interest in them if they become pregnant or grow old or ill. This is instead of being nominally oppressed by husbands who are supposed to keep them for life, for better or worse, for richer or poorer, in sickness and in health. A campaign originally aimed at allowing the greater personal fulfilment of women, and their liberation from drudgery, has replaced one form of drudgery with another, much harder to escape and more ruthless. And a campaign which had been supposed to allow women to be more free is now a campaign which requires the dismantling of private life, where free thought is nurtured and independent, thinking individuals are brought up.

But this is the part of the change which pleases the extreme revolutionaries. They are not old-fashioned Marxists who worry about the living conditions of the workers. All that is finished, along with the sealed coalmines and silent shipyards. They are in pursuit of the pure and utopian revolutionary aims which walked for a while alongside working-class socialism, and now have fallen out of step with it. In the great wealthy nations of North America and Europe, the objective of the revolutionaries is to destroy and expunge the restraints placed upon human selfishness by the Christian religion. The permanent married family is the greatest single obstacle to this project. The opportunity to persuade women to become brides of the state, or brides of capital, is the greatest chance these campaigners have ever had.

Under Stalin, the peoples of Russia and the Warsaw Pact countries endured but survived direct attacks upon religion, marriage and the family – because these were frontal assaults in which the enemy was plain and his aim clear. In the free countries, the attack has taken the form of a seduction, the creation of a parallel form of life whose instant attractions conceal its dangers. In this new world, women do not marry for life (for this is unendurable imprisonment). They do not raise their own children (for this is a form of enslavement which destroys their potential). They denounce any calls for them to obey their husbands out of love (for this is feudal oppression), but readily obey workplace masters for money. In return they are rewarded with that money and the sort of pleasures that can be bought with money. But they live in growing fear of age, as demonstrated by the disturbing fashions for Botox treatment and plastic surgery. For, unlike lifelong marriage, employment depends on youth. And so does the availability of sexual fulfilment, supposedly made so much simpler by the new morality.

Sexual relations between men and women have become a mistrustful maze, with many women fearing rape and many men fearing that they will be accused of it in courts where independent evidence will not exist and the jury will have to judge between two rival accounts of the same event. On a more mundane level, women may desire marriage. And so do many men. But the laws which now govern wedlock ensure that many men will avoid a contract which can be easily broken by one party against the wishes of the other, which can strip them of much of their wealth and deprive them of their children. Also, the former importance of marriage has been dissolved by general sexual availability without commitment. Once men had to marry for sexual satisfaction. Now they do not. Women have robbed themselves, by choosing easily available sex, of the great bargaining power which they used to possess during a few short, desirable years.

The children of this confusion, often drugged to make them behave, are brought up by strangers or by the state. They frequently have distant relations with their parents and learn little or nothing from them except mistrust. In British society in the last few decades, a number of things have simply stopped. Girls no longer learn to sew and bake. Boys no longer play rough games and in many cases play no sport either. Children do not sing. Most of the young know no history or lore of the past. Local accents, except for a few very powerful ones, have faded and died. Nursery rhymes and proverbs are unknown, street games such as hopscotch and conkers have nearly vanished, ancient slang expressions have been forgotten in favour of the English of the soap opera. Simple, clearly understood religion of almost all types, no longer learned at mothers' knees, has evaporated so that most of the young have no idea what happens in churches or how to behave if they enter one. These are the symptoms of a much deeper loss. The destruction of private family life has dried up a thousand-year-old river of myth and language, custom and morals, poetry and story. The riverbed has, as such ravaged places do, filled up with the rubbish and refuse chucked into young minds by TV programmes and computer games.

And we have, growing among us, a citizenry prepared for enslavement, ignorant of its origins, past, rights, traditions and duties, wholly at the mercy of anyone who can get control of the transmitters. This is a terrible thing, a scandal just as bad as the sending of children up chimneys or down coalmines two hundred years ago. I do not believe that the British Left wanted such a result, though I suspect it may be pleasing to some of the further-fetched supporters of the birth-control fanatic Margaret Sanger, the incest-obsessed Sigmund Freud, the mistaken advocate of value-free sex Margaret Mead, or the sex maniacs Alfred Kinsey or Wilhelm Reich. Yet the Left continues to behave as if these changes are both beneficial and unavoidable. And the supposed forces of conservatism are either too complacent or too afraid to oppose this extraodinarily radical social revolution. Only in a wholly broken political system could there be such a need for reform, and no reformers ready to address it.

10

Equality or Tolerance?
One or the Other, but Not Both

Of course the persecution of the sexually unconventional is wrong in general. It is wrong because it is personally cruel and a misuse of public law to police private life. The difficult task is how to design rules under which such people can live at peace in a society which generally does not approve of their actions, disdains their way of life and often dislikes their moral choice. Nearly as difficult is deciding where the boundary lies between the tolerable and the intolerable.

We now agree that homosexual adults should be free to live together as couples untroubled by the law. This is tolerance, as recommended by the Wolfenden Report and passed into law in 1967. It would be hard to find anyone who seriously objects to it – precisely because it wisely makes sexual preference a private matter.

As was the case with ultra-feminism, the Left of the 1960s and 1970s was not especially vocal about homosexuality. Homosexual politicians of the Left were wise to keep their tastes to themselves, because their own political parties would not have wished to defend them if they had been exposed.

Leo Abse's necessary law reform in 1967 had abolished the indefensible old sex laws, rightly known as the 'blackmailer's charter'. The central words of this compromise – 'between consenting adults in private' – seemed to sum up reasonable conditions under which homosexual acts could take place and those who did them could be left alone. The entirely different campaign for equality, for ever lower ages of consent, for legal privileges for homosexual unions, had not then connected itself with the radical Left and would not have won much support among most of us if it had, judging by the general use of coarse and abusive terms for homosexuals in casual conversation among sixties Left-wingers. And not just among them, or then. In the early 1990s I personally heard (but alas did not record, or I should name him) a political figure much revered by many on the Left making crude remarks about the broadcaster and academic Dr David Starkey, along the lines of 'I've never liked queers'. Other traces remain of the disgusted, harsh attitudes which were once considered normal by those of all political views. There is a passage in the 1950s novel *No Love for Johnnie* by the Left-wing Labour MP Wilfred Fienburgh in which a homosexual young man is portrayed with some loathing. 'I've got to get away,' thinks the socialist hero, as he recoils from the effeminate, high-pitched youth. Rather later, in Frederick Forsyth's 1971 thriller *The Day of the Jackal*, the would-be assassin evades three police checks because the gendarmes are portrayed as being so revolted by his disguise – a heavily made-up male prostitute – that they do not bother to check his papers.

Once again the Left of today have made a shocking leap of logic from one wholly reasonable and just position to another much more contentious one. Yet they have sought to pretend that the one is the same as the other. Those who (as I did and still do) supported the 1967 compromise, on the grounds of tolerance, are accused of intolerance if they now decline to support civil partnerships (as I do), or provisions to ban discrimination on the grounds of homosexual orientation. They are also condemned if they resist adoption of children by homosexual couples or object to schools equating homosexual relationships with heterosexual marriage. There are interesting arguments to be had over all these reforms – but surely it is clear that they are nothing to do with tolerance. Tolerance, after all, implies disapproval.

There would be no need to tolerate acts or rules which you did not dislike, or to which you were indifferent.

Yet increasingly conventional wisdom and intellectual fashion frown angrily on those who oppose these ideas, and it cannot be long before those who dissent from them are excluded from debate by disapproval and intolerance. It is all very well for people like me, with platforms in national newspapers, to disagree with such ideas. But powerless individuals are not so free. A town hall registrar has already faced official disapproval for declining to officiate at homosexual civil partnerships (see the 2008 case of Lillian Ladele and Islington Council) and teachers or other public officials who express open doubts about such things expose themselves to career damage and possible actions under anti-discrimination laws which equate discrimination over 'sexual orientation' with racial bigotry. There is very little tolerance here, and one of the striking features of the sexual revolution is that, while being conducted in the name of tolerance, it is wholly intolerant as soon as it is strong enough to punish its opponents.

Civil partnerships are troubling to moral conservatives partly because they (along with homosexual adoption and the approval of homosexual acts in official sex education programmes) place dissident public servants (and others) in danger of this liberal intolerance. The extraordinary case of the Bournemouth preacher, the late Harry Hammond, prosecuted and convicted for denouncing homosexuality in a public square, is recounted in my *Abolition of Liberty* for any who think that this problem does not exist. But that is not really the root of the trouble. The real problem is that these unions are revolutionary actions dressed up as acts of personal kindness, hard for decent people to oppose yet – once in place – deeply subversive of the existing order. They are clearly a form of civil marriage, given a less contentious name to avoid political trouble.

They are legally almost identical to civil marriage and confer its benefits. Increasingly, and crucially, they also receive the same status and regard. The partners hold celebrations which mimic those of marriage, and often seek the blessing of the Church as well. Yet (unlike civil marriages) they are wholly different from Christian marriage. They require a specifically homosexual union, being denied to two brothers or two sisters living together. They are by definition not linked to procreation. They are also not necessary for the compassionate purposes which are often claimed for them. Where hospitals and other public institutions declined to accept a homosexual lover as next of kin, then specific laws could have been passed to overcome this. The same goes for tenancy agreements when one member of a homosexual couple dies. Problems over inheritance could have been resolved by abolishing inheritance tax or greatly raising its threshold, which has in fact now happned'.

Their real purpose is clear. It is 'propaganda of the deed', a legal change which makes it clear that from now on the union of two men or two women is equivalent to Christian marriage between a man and a woman. This crucially redistributes the special privileges of marriage to others. If privileges are not exclusive, they cease to be privileges. Marriage requires privileges because it is full of perils and difficult to sustain, and needs to be defended against the many forces which constantly threaten to break up individual marriages and to dethrone marriage from its position in society. This is a secondary but important part of the general cultural and legal assault on lifelong marriage which the state and the sixties generation have been mounting for the last fifty years (see my *Abolition of Britain*).

Civil partnerships have another useful function in the culture war. The instinctive opponent of such unions, who can see that there is something amiss here but cannot quite work out what it is, can easily be corralled as an unkind and intolerant bigot. This – the classification of dissent as a phobia or a pathology, not worthy of rebuttal but only of personal contempt – is the usual response of the new establishment to any objections to the sexual revolution. Opposition to state subsidies to unwed mothers is misrepresented as hostility to those mothers and their children. Opposition to the equalisation of hedonistic temporary sexual unions and procreative lifelong marriages is characterised as a phobia against individual homosexuals, or as a personal slight to an umarried couple, and so on. Distress at divorce long ago became almost unspeakable because of the large number of divorcees and the fear that they would be 'offended' by the expression of this view.

It is partly because of the gross dishonesty of these tactics that it is necessary for conservatives to continue to state their case in spite of the defamation they will inevitably suffer as a result.

In fact, there is probably more tolerance – and more disapproval – going on than most are prepared to admit in the open. I strongly suspect that many of those on the Left now happy to howl 'homophobe' at sexual conservatives would be privately distressed and disturbed to find a child of their own embarking on a homosexual relationship below the age of 21, and none too pleased if a child of theirs chose (or otherwise arrived at) homosexuality at any age. I also think many of them would privately share Matthew Parris's view (see below) that impressionable young people may be influenced into making lifelong sexual choices which might not be inevitable.

The new reforms, for better or worse, are not a logical or moral continuation of the old ones. Just as Lord Macpherson's embrace of openly racialist policing marks a break with 1960s multiracial Leftism, the new campaign to suppress expressions of 'homophobia' is distinct from 1960s tolerance. In fact it is in many ways its opposite, since it actively seeks to suppress certain forms of behaviour which it does not like. It does not seek tolerance for its own practices – total equality of legal status and also of esteem are required. It does not offer tolerance to its opponents – total acquiescence to the new morality is required. This is not – yet – a reversed blackmailers' charter, but it may soon be the case that opinions expressed in private may be publicised to destroy the careers of individuals. The opportunities this provides for unscrupulous pressure are worrying in themselves. But the important fact is that we seem unable to stop in the middle, but must move from intolerance of homosexuals to intolerance of sexual conservatives.

The tolerance of 1967 was an act of reform, not of revolution, removing a law which wrongly used the penal code to enforce a moral rule. That law encouraged an equivalent evil by allowing blackmailers to prosper, and intervened quite needlessly in private matters where conscience, not law, should be supreme. There is no organic or logical connection between this reform and the later, revolutionary, attempt to alter the moral culture of the country. It is quite possible to be entirely in favour of Leo Abse's Act while resisting the idea that homosexual relations should have equal or similar standing with heterosexual marriages. It is totally consistent to support Abse's tolerance while resisting the persecution of individuals with moral objections to homosexual acts.

Many of Abse's supporters specifically warned at the time that their votes were conditional on the age of consent remaining at 21. They judged that unformed adolescents needed some sort of legal protection from being influenced by their elders. Though derided nowadays, the argument still deserves thoughtful consideration. In a characteristically honest article on the sexual spectrum (*The Times*, 6 August 2006), the self-acknowledged homosexual Matthew Parris wrote 'I think sexuality is a supple as well as subtle thing, and can sometimes be influenced, even promoted; I think that in some people some drives can be discouraged and others encouraged; I think some people can choose.' If this is true, and if it is true that adolescents are impressionable (which it is) then surely there is an argument for an age of consent higher than 16?

The real problem, for those who would overturn the Christian moral order, is not whether it might be true that the young could be influenced into homosexual acts, habits and milieux. The problem is that this possibility could be seen as a danger rather than an opportunity. Thus the very suggestion that it might be worse if that young man chose a homosexual orientation rather than a heterosexual one is the real offence against the new code of belief. The new order is based upon the idea that there is no moral distinction between homosexual and heterosexual acts, that those who believe that there is are morally faulty, and that the human race can be educated out of its general disapproval of homosexual acts. This is a revolutionary, not a tolerant or liberal position. Do those who support it, claiming they do so in the name of tolerance, realise the radicalism of the programme they are supporting? I suspect not.

Of course the first obligation of wealth and power is to defend the poor and the weak. It is quite clear that political correctness has succeeded so well because of the strong appeal to many people of the simple good manners which it enforces. I believe – and it gets me into trouble with those who generally agree with me – that the n-word is as unfit for public use as the f-word, and should not, for instance, be transmitted on prime-time TV. I think it is quite reasonable of TV companies to cut the scene in the film the *The Dam Busters* in which the dog called 'N*****' features. I think this because I suspect that quite a lot of bigoted people gain pleasure from seeing this unpleasant word transmitted on national TV. I do not think golliwogs can any longer be regarded as innocent toys. I have encountered too many racial bigots who are enthusiastic owners of golliwog dolls or badges to think that this is so.

The Left was right about these things at a time when the Right was wrong. It deserves credit, while the Right ought to feel shame about the unhappiness and hurt it failed to prevent. Many conservatives continue to defend crass bad manners in such things, though in some cases they do this only because they think that they are opposing an oppressive conformism.

The Left were right about many other things. They were right about the railways, when Conservatives supported the destruction of a national possession. Their failure to do anything at all about it makes their opposition less impressive.

But at least they knew it was wrong. I increasingly suspect the Left were right about the sale of council houses, a measure still enthusiastically endorsed by Tory Party members from Michael Heseltine to Margaret Thatcher. The break-up of a settled society on these estates, the disappearance of authority in their streets, must have played some part in the social collapse that now afflicts many such places. It is also hard to see why the giant, suspect extravaganza of housing benefit is superior to the generally honest system of subsidised rents. Tories might also ask themselves why it was conservative to make what were in effect large state grants of wealth to council tenants, so allowing them to enter the housing market ahead of private tenants and others who had saved their own money towards deposits.

The Left are right to put part of the blame for the current riot of selfishness on the shoulders of Lady Thatcher. They are wrong to distort her remark that there 'is no such thing as society' to mean something it plainly did not. But they are right to perceive a moral emptiness in her government, which showed no interest in moral or cultural issues, in family breakdown, the decay of marriage, the collapse of discipline and learning in schools, in all its eighteen years in office.

The Left also has a better record on the great European issue than the Right. The best and most powerful speech in opposition to British entry to the (then) Common Market was made by Hugh Gaitskell on 2 October 1962, when he said 'We must be clear about this: it does mean, if this is the idea, the end of Britain as an independent European state. I make no apology for repeating it. It means the end of a thousand years of history.' The then Tory Prime Minister, Harold Macmillan, responded to this accurate warning a few days later with nothing more than a feeble joke, and continued his spurned attempts to join, which would in the end succeed under his successor, Edward Heath, with the keen support of *his* successor, Margaret Thatcher. She would not recognise the problem until the last months of her premiership, and was destroyed by her own party largely because she had begun to adopt Hugh Gaitskell's position. It is worth adding, for those who have forgotten that a patriotic Left ever existed in this country, that Gaitskell and Aneurin Bevan share the joint honours for making the most powerful, courageous and passionate defences of an independent British nuclear capability.

And, while recent years have witnessed a tiresome political struggle over the corpse of George Orwell, I am happy to accept that he is the property of the Left, provided that they accept that his social conservatism and his love of his country were until recently part of their tradition as well as mine. If they now reject these things, then they have less of a claim to Orwell than they did before.

Labour's almost complete swoon into the arms of the European Union (a few short years after campaigning for an exit from the EU) is one of the most extraordinary, and least inspected, political turnarounds of modern history. It is also one of the consequences of the new, denatured politics of the 'Centre Left', in which the range of permitted views in any major party has become so narrow that almost no dissent of any kind is permitted.

One of the great unexamined political mysteries of the last forty years is the puzzle of where what used to be called 'Right Wing Labour' has gone. Once, Labour Cabinet members voted to retain the death penalty, Labour MPs opposed abortion and resisted easy divorce. Even more strikingly, Labour was once the party that supported grammar schools. Now even avowedly Roman Catholic Labour MPs and ministers do not actively oppose abortion and divorce, but merely seek personal dispensation from having to support them. They insist that they are no longer political questions, but matters of private conscience in which they wish to beg to be excused from voting for policies their forebears would have fought.

This atrophy of religion and patriotism in the Labour Party, like the atrophy of the same things in the Tory Party, is the deep problem beneath all others. It is the absence of anyone who will articulate these feelings which has encouraged the consensus of expediency which is politely called the 'Centre Left'. Freed from higher obligations of either kind, the politician has nothing to keep him from becoming the servant of his own political class, and a pursuer of the line of least resistance.

11

The Fall of the Meritocracy

Why would a socialist support a school system that ensured that the children of the rich and influential were privileged, while the offspring of the poor and weak were deprived? Since this is the system that we have, and since socialists do support it, and with some vigour, it is amazing that this question is not asked more often. All around us we see evidence of it, and the personal behaviour of many senior Labour politicians when they come to choose their children's schools, tricky, dishonest and self-serving, is a reliable source of embarrassing scandals. These events play for a little while in the press, flare, flicker and die. Like so much of the news in our country today, such stories only fulfil half their purpose.

News is meant to shock, because it reveals a state of affairs that is plainly wrong. Normally, that wrong is in some way righted or at least expiated, once it has been exposed. If it is the disclosure of a crime, the story usually ends with the arrest, trial and punishment of a culprit. If it is the revelation of an injustice to an individual or a group, it generally ends in some sort of restitution. Fat cats are forced to ration their cream. Dirty hospitals are made to clean their filthy lavatories and scrub their bloodstained floors. Sordid broadcasters are forced off the air. The monarchy, found to be privileged, is compelled to pay tax and to forgo much of its privilege and grandeur. But if it is the exposure of socialist hypocrisy and privilege, there are no consequences. The hypocrisy is allowed to continue and is soon afterwards repeated elsewhere by others. A Prime Minister whose government disapproves of school selection sends his sons to a selective school. One of his ministers sends her child to a grammar school, a type of establishment so loathed by the Labour Party that it has banned the creation of any more such schools by the law of the land. A leading Labour Party figure moves house expensively to get his daughters into the catchment area of a rare good girls-only state secondary school. A Left-wing MP sends her son to a public school and is frank and unapologetic about it. An ambitious lawyer cannot get selected for a Labour seat because he sends his children to private schools. So he is made a lord and becomes a minister anyway. Nobody seems to learn anything from any of these events, except to cover his tracks more effectively next time.

In this one field, the national drama stutters and stalls, without a conclusion or a catharsis – and it does so repeatedly. I believe that this is because the political, cultural, educational and moral elite in this country put egalitarian social policy before education. They are not prepared to recognise the extent of their own error in public (though they are fully aware of it in private. It would be interesting to know how many of the generally 'progressive' education journalists in this country have made use of the same tricks, dodges and wangles as have 'progressive' politicians). They avoid the consequences of their own ideas by buying or using privilege to obtain special privileges for their own offspring. When caught, they angrily turn on those who have found them out, accusing them of invading their privacy. Useless to point out to them that, by their own decisions, they daily invade the private lives of others who do not have the skill or the means to manipulate the state education system in this way.

It is also strange verging on astonishing that almost nobody can see any contradiction in this. The intelligent and highly educated are in many ways the worst. Read these words, spoken by history professor Peter Hennessy on BBC Radio 4's *Any Questions* on 11 August 2006 in a discussion on whether

British school examinations have been diluted. Having revealed that he had himself been a grammar school pupil, he continued his contribution with a partisan attack on the Conservatives for 'having a vested interest in being mean-spirited about other people's life chances'. He went on to say:

> And when you think – when you think when I went to college – when Jonathan [Dimbleby] and I went to college, because we're much of an age, 7 per cent of the age group went to college, it's now 43 per cent, I don't think it should get any wider. But ... it's reached parts, like Heineken Lager, that the system never reached in my day. We have wonderful mature students, we have a lot locally recruited from the East End ... because of the Robbins Report, we were told more would mean worse. That was before 10 per cent of the age group went. Now what did that tell you about the attitudes of that society? That the divine spark – the divine spark of education, intellectual curiosity, does not depend on the socioeconomic status of the loins that bring us into this world.

Professor Hennessy's statement verges on the incoherent. The percentage attending higher education colleges cannot possibly be a measure of the numbers who possess the 'divine spark of intellectual curiosity'. It is a measure of how many places can be provided at such colleges, and how affordable and worthwhile it is for those who gain the places – many of them vocational rather than academic – to take them up. It entirely avoids the question of whether a system which provides such places to 43 per cent of the population can even remotely be compared to one which provides places for 7 per cent. If his argument, that wider access means the encouragement of ever more divine sparks, is true, then why should he believe that 43 per cent is the upper limit, as he says he does? How is this percentage arrived at? Is it not perhaps true that only a small number of people are capable of benefiting from true higher education, and that it would therefore be wise to select them on merit rather than by the size of their parents' bank accounts?

An interestingly contrasting view came a few days later from Baroness Warnock, another much-respected member of the liberal establishment, with an amazing partial admission, in the *Observer* of 20 August 2006. Predicting that Oxford and Cambridge would soon drop out of the top ten of world universities, she said that one reason for this would be

> [T]he concept of learning, the acquisition of knowledge and the exercise of creative imagination within the constraints of evidence and reason, has been almost fatally devalued. To see how this happened, one has to look to the schools from which university students come.
>
> There is a mismatch within educational policy between the desire to make education the means by which pupils may be enabled to earn their living in a way that uses their abilities and contributes to the country's economy and the desire to turn more of them than ever before into graduates. The silliest thing Tony Blair ever said was that 50 per cent of the school population should go on to university.

Lady Warnock went on to argue for implementation of the contentious Tomlinson Report on examinations. I will not attempt to deal with this argument here. But what is interesting is the admission by a member of the liberal establishment that there has been an anti-elitist bias in education policy, and her repudiation of that policy. This is a far more creditable response to this problem than Professor Hennessy's partisan bluster, which offers a broad avenue to mediocrity to the ordinary and the brilliant alike. Lady Warnock said:

> This abhorrence of an elite lies at the very heart of our educational troubles, first at school, then at university. Yet how could we possibly hope that our universities might

become world class if we did not think that they were elitist? Most rational people would accept, as a matter of manifest fact, that not everyone can be a Nobel Prize winner. But though they accept that, they then go on, half-automatically, to suggest that everyone should be given the chance to become a laureate.

This is morally unexceptionable, but does not mean that everyone should go to university. It means, rather, that everyone from the age of five should be given an education that enables them to exercise their exceptional talents, if such they have. This, in turn, entails that if there are those who show academic prowess, they should be given the tools, such as a command of language and rational argument, with which they can progress, and they should sit examinations, success in which will prove to the world that they are good at their work.

I believe the Tomlinson recommendations would gradually have ensured that. We might have escaped from the confusion between social and intellectual discrimination.

Many doubt that Tomlinson would solve the problem. Many do not think that five is the right age to begin school. But the heart of Lady Warnock's argument is at least sound. An elite is necessary and right in education. The problems arise in how to select it, and in what happens to those who do not qualify for it.

Left-wing reformers demolished a functioning selective secondary school system that picked its winners at an age – 11 years old – when good teaching can easily discover and polish talent, and rescue the neglected and the ill-taught before it is too late. They did this on the grounds that it was unfair to condemn anyone to official second-class status. The same reformers have managed to create a university system, whose degrees are increasingly essential for any kind of middle-class trade or profession. Entry to that system is coldly and unforgivingly selective at a point in life where class and wealth have already done most of their work and where it is extremely difficult to make up for years eaten by the locusts of ignorance and indiscipline. It is not even an openly tripartite division, as the destroyed selective secondary system was. Oxford and Cambridge are special. A few other universities are rated as excellent, but in real life their graduates know that Oxbridge competitors will always be preferred to them. More are mediocre, and many others are plain bad but many applicants have almost no means of discovering the truth about the colleges and courses they will enter. Compulsory failure has simply been moved a few years further on in life and is more unjust than ever before. Its victims have to pay for it, and may have to suffer three years of neglect at a bad university before they find out exactly how worthless it has been to them.

The only response of the 'progressive consensus' to this obvious inequality is to conclude that if good education is only available to a minority then it would be better if it were not available at all. They seek to destroy the ability of the best universities to select the best students, a process which will in the end reduce them to the level of the rest. Yet this is dressed in the crusading rhetoric of fairness. During the 2005 election, the Liberal Democrat education spokesman, Phil Willis, defended his party's opposition to charging student fees by saying – with much justice – that university places should be won by merit, not money. I asked him why, in that case, his party supported a system which ensured that selection to the best secondary schools was decided by money and influence rather than merit. He was unable to give a coherent answer. Nobody (except me) reported the exchange.

Despite all this organised lying and fumbling, there is a dawning of understanding on the intelligent Left which may yet lead to something, though such boldness often gets those responsible into trouble with the thought police who patrol the frontiers of legitimate debate, and who decide who is a good person and who a bad one. Perhaps the most striking and candid epiphany has been that of Nick Cohen, the *Observer* columnist who in most respects is aligned with the Left (and about whom I shall have more to say). Cohen recently revealed how he had been discussing the schooling of his child with similarly Leftist colleagues. To begin with they urged him to move to an area with good state schools. But that was not all. Cohen wrote:

> The principled objection seemed obvious. If parents with money moved in, the cost of housing would rise, driving young working-class parents out of the catchment area. They conceded I was right, but held firm to the main point: selection by the ability to buy an expensive house was acceptable. Selection by the ability to pay expensive school fees was not. The boy arrived in the world, his cries drowned by the noise of ever-weirder advice. The most unlikely people revealed that they had been born again when their first child was born and urged me to find the Lord.
>
> 'You must go to church at once.'
>
> 'But I haven't been to church in years.'
>
> 'Get back in there now. I did and my daughter is now at the Catholic primary.'
>
> 'But you're a revolutionary socialist. You don't believe in God.'
>
> 'Of course I don't believe in God. I just lie to the priest like everyone else.'
>
> I learnt that not only was selection by house price acceptable, selection by the ability to con vicars was fine as well. It's fortunate that those doing the lying don't believe. If they did, they would spend the rest of their lives in fear of eternal hell fire.

Cohen went on to quote a *London Evening Standard* report that the premiums paid on houses in the catchment areas of good state schools over otherwise identical houses a few streets away were hitting 70 per cent.

Cohen was later accused in the *Observer* letters page of turning into me, a charge verging on the defamatory in the world in which he lives. Others get into different kinds of trouble – far worse than the mild embarrassment that Labour ministers get into for playing the system. Stephen Pollard, a Labour supporter, was working for the Fabian Society when he sought to publish a pamphlet advocating a return to selection by ability by state secondary schools (*Schools, Selection and the Left*, eventually brought out by the Social Market Foundation in October 1995). He was prevented from issuing it under the Fabian imprint, and in the end lost his position at the Society as a result. Even so, he persisted, and still persists. Another sharp Left-wing critic, himself a member of the comprehensive generation, is Robert Crampton, who wrote in *The Times* in May 2006: 'On this issue, dogma is far more powerful than reason or evidence. How else to explain how a large section of the Labour Party is now more antipathetic towards selection by ability than selection by income?' I quote his article almost in its entirety because, coming from such a source, it seems to me to be heartrending in its sense of lost opportunity and its keen recognition of the contradictory position of the Labour MP's standard support for comprehensive schools:

It really is bizarre that your average Labour rebel, often the personal beneficiary of a selective education, dislikes grammar schools, or whatever Tony Blair and Andrew Adonis are trying to rebrand them as at the moment, more than he does public schools. But this has long been the Labour way. Before Tony Crosland came along, all but the most prestigious public schools were withering on the vine. Now, 40 years on from 10/65 [the Crosland circular pressing local authorities to introduce Comprehensives], the biggest transmitters of privilege in Britain are booming again. Clever move, Labour Party! Another blow for social equality.

Mr Crampton recalled:

I went to a large, streamed comprehensive in a suburb of Hull in the late Seventies. My class formed part of the top stream. We were the sons and daughters of lecturers, trawlermen, teachers, sales reps, a painter and decorator, engineers, repairmen. A wide social mix. We arrived bright-eyed and keen, and we left, five or seven years later, well entertained, but not especially well educated. Yeah, we had a laugh, but we didn't learn much. Enough to get by. Your status depended on your looks, your athleticism and your willingness to be disruptive. Academic ability was an irrelevance at best, a hindrance at worst.

There were 35 children in my O-level class. After those exams, half the class, particularly those from more working-class backgrounds, voted with their feet and left. They had the grades to stay on; no one encouraged them to do so. Quite the opposite in some cases. And of the half of my class who went into the sixth form, only half of them went on to university, a dismal return. Again, it was the working-class kids who bailed out.

Now, in a previous generation, or had we lived in a different LEA (Local Education Authority), my class would have gone en masse to a grammar school. When I think about this, I ask myself three questions. Would we have received a better education at a grammar? (The usual argument in favour of selection.) Would the rest of our school, the 70 per cent not in the top stream, have been worse off if we hadn't been around? (The usual argument against selection.) And (I ask this only when feeling especially public-spirited) which option would have most benefited the country?

The answer to the first question, as everyone knows, is yes. Even many opponents of grammars accept they were better for bright children than comprehensives have proved to be. The elite ethos, the raised expectations, the decreased likelihood of some strutting psychopath assaulting you in the lavatories at dinnertime, grammars were conducive to the stretching of minds and the pursuit of excellence.

Not surprising, this: they were designed to make pupils feel special; comprehensives weren't.

The people I've met who went to grammars learnt in greater depth and breadth than I did. Their lessons were more rigorous and more challenging. Roy Jenkins? Denis Healey? Harold Wilson? I don't think they were baking sheets of paper in the oven to make them look like medieval parchment for history homework in the Thirties, as I was 40-odd years on.

If we would have benefited from being elsewhere, would the rest of the school have suffered? I can't see how. The top stream had no academic, and precious little social, contact with the other streams. The mechanism by which our presence was supposed to raise the overall standard did not exist. If anything, having the top stream monopolise not only the academic life of the school, but also its sporting, musical and dramatic efforts, must have been demoralising. If we hadn't been there, those otherwise in the middle of the ability range would have been at its top.

By a roundabout route, after A-level retakes elsewhere, I got to Oxford. I sized up the other undergraduates, the majority of them from fee-paying or selective state schools, and I knew that the ten or twelve cleverest kids in my class at school would have had nothing to fear from them in terms of pure intellect.

Nothing. But most of my classmates hadn't even applied. Those that had, hadn't made it. But it wasn't prejudice that kept them out. It was that the other candidates, the ones from selective schools, were better prepared, better coached, better educated. Gordon Brown, take note. It wasn't that Laura Spence's [a student refused entry to Oxford whose case Mr Brown took up] rivals were cleverer than she was. It was that they almost certainly knew more and could express it better.

The people I was at school with have done OK. That's what they always say about bright kids in comps, isn't it? Oh, they'll be OK. But we haven't done as well as we could have done if we hadn't been – there's no polite way of putting this – shafted by Labour ideology for the past 40 years. The people I was at Oxford with, meanwhile, they're running the country, some deservedly so, others not. How do you want to choose your elite? By family connections? By what your dad earned? Or by ability?

They should consider this, these Labour men and women who detest their leader and educational selection in equal measure. For more than 30 years, from the death of Hugh Gaitskell to the death of John Smith, when the grammar school generation was on stream, the Labour Party did not feel the need to choose a public schoolboy for its leader. Since 1994, when the comprehensive generation started to become available, they've had Blair from Fettes, and soon they'll have Brown, the product of a ruthlessly selective fast-track education. And before too long, I suspect, we'll have Cameron from Eton. He'll be that school's nineteenth Prime Minister.

We're still waiting for the comprehensive system to produce its first.

Francis Gilbert, author of *I'm a Teacher, Get Me Out of Here* (Short Books, London, 2004) also showed some bravery by writing in the *Guardian* of 10 August 2004 that 'adhering to a non-selective system has created ghettoisation in urban schools. Many are dominated by one social or ethnic group. Giving schools the power to select pupils is a good way round this.'

Mr Gilbert noted that, thirty years after the Comprehensive Revolution swept through British secondary education, most of the (Labour) Cabinet were 'either public-school educated or from grammar schools'.

Like Robert Crampton, he wondered where the comprehensive generation, from which so much should have been expected if the experiment had succeeded, had gone. He asked:

Isn't it disturbing to see that very few comprehensive pupils, especially ones from working-class backgrounds, have made their mark on society? Look at the upper echelons of the BBC, or the media, or the legal system, and you will see that they are dominated by people from public schools and grammars.

He is right. And where comprehensive pupils have succeeded in the professions, it is generally because their schools have been exceptional in some way, covertly selective in one of the many ways available.

It is fascinating to look through *Dod's Parliamentary Companion*, which lists the educational backgrounds of MPs, and see how many Labour MPs went to grammar schools or their Scottish equivalents. It is also interesting that they often half-conceal this by vaguely giving the school's name without making clear that it *was* a grammar school. One even pretends that his 1950s secondary modern was a comprehensive (I checked with the local education authority, who readily confirmed that they had no comprehensives when he claimed to have attended one, or for several years afterwards), so ideologically committed is he to the 'comprehensive ideal'. Even more curious is the behaviour of some Tory MPs. Theresa May, an ambitious Tory, declares that her school was a comprehensive, but a little checking discloses that it was a grammar school when she first went there, and only became a comprehensive in her final years. There is no-one still at the school who remembers the precise details. Without a doubt, it would have kept much of the atmosphere and many of the methods of a grammar school until she left.

What is it about comprehensive schools that makes Labour and Tory politicians alike pretend to have attended them when they didn't? Why is sending children to state schools viewed as virtuous in itself? The current Conservative leader, David Cameron, says that he hopes to send his children to state schools. He has managed to obtain a place for his daughter, Nancy, at a small and over-subscribed Anglican primary school some distance from his home. He has never been asked why, and so has not explained why. But it seems likely that, just as Labour politicians feel the need to appear to be egalitarian, the new de-natured Tory Party now has the same need. Michael Gove, Mr Cameron's friend and ally, and also (at the time of writing) the Shadow Education Secretary, has also managed to obtain a place at the same school for one of his children. Both men's wives are active in producing the parish magazine of the church to which this school is connected, and both men have been observed attending divine service there. Let us hope the spiritual benefits of this association have been great.

Mass self-deception about schools is one of the strangest aspects of modern education, and is not confined to politicians and public figures. Thousands of people make a great effort to give a false impression about where their children are going to school. As many middle-class parents know – the Blairs among them – there is a good deal of secret selection in the officially comprehensive school system. The simplest way to take advantage of this, if you happen to have money, is to move into the catchment area of one of the few remaining first-rate state schools, usually former grammar schools. This was what one powerful and wealthy London Left-wing couple did. They relocated from Bayswater to Camden, at enormous cost, so that their daughters could attend the Camden School for Girls, whose catchment area is roughly a quarter of a mile from the school gates. They have now moved away again. Another rich Labour couple, one a senior minister, the other a lawyer, also sent a daughter to this far-from-typical state school. The fact that it is a state school, and officially a comprehensive, as far as they are concerned, completely outweighs the fact that most London parents of any class would have almost no hope of winning a place there, and the price of houses in its tiny catchment area is enormous.

Fiona Millar, herself a former grammar-school girl (Camden School for Girls, in its openly selective days), has established herself as a prominent advocate of comprehensive education. She rails against middle-class parents who shun the state system.

But she but just happens to live in the (once again) very small catchment area of two of London's best and least typical comprehensive schools. This could explain her failure to condemn this particular method of obtaining advantage in the system, while appearing to support the comprehensive principle. She is, by contrast, scathing about those who gain advantage through religion or through selection by ability. Another deception of this kind is the introduction of 'sixth form colleges' (often former grammar schools) which rely on the disappearance of non-academic pupils at the age of 16 and can function as selective schools without actually having to keep anyone out – except of course for the usual victims, the clever children from poor homes whose parents do not appreciate the value of education and are not prepared to pay for the keep of teenage boys and girls who could be going out to work. In some cases they simply decline to teach the vocational courses which children from poorer homes tend to follow. But this only gets rid of a minority. Such pupils will almost invariably have been driven away from education already by the poor discipline and low standards of ordinary comprehensives in poor areas. Several continental countries, having been forced by political fashion to abandon selection, have used this method to achieve covert segregation of the classes higher up the ladder of age. It is an old idea. In Stalin's Soviet Union in the 1930s, fees were charged for academic secondary schooling, so excluding most of the children of the supposedly supreme working class.

The next simplest way, if you happen to be a Roman Catholic, is to get your children into a selective religious foundation. As Francis Gilbert puts it:

> 'Faith-based' schools such as the London Oratory can select pupils on the basis of their religious orientation. In practice, this means that headteachers can interview children and glean much information about their academic abilities as well as their commitment to a faith. 'Faith-based' school is code for 'selective' school, for those in the know.

Oxbridge colleges become very coy when asked to identify the state schools from which they take undergraduates. I wrote to many of them in 2004 asking for this information, and was amused and impressed by the variety of feeble excuses they put up to avoid answering my questions. Of those that replied at all, most hid behind ridiculous excuses about confidentiality and data protection, even when I made it perfectly clear that I was not seeking details of individual students and that I would not even name individual schools, let alone identify pupils. Oxford is now under pressure to increase its state school intake from about 55 per cent to 77 per cent, by what amounts to positive discrimination in favour of state school entrants. It is easy to see why the colleges do not want too much scrutiny of how they achieve this, since if they wish to keep up any sort of standard they are going to have to get most of their new state entry from grammar schools and from the secretly selective schools – which officially do not exist.

Before the mass abolition of grammar schools in the late 1960s, the old universities were far more willing to discuss this, and no wonder, since the entrance to these places has never been fairer or more transparent, before or since. The Franks Report on Oxford University, published in 1966, found that a revolution had happened as a result of the opening of the grammar schools to all, and the linked expansion of direct grant places at private schools, after World War II. In 1938–9, independent school pupils won 62 per cent of places at Oxford. Of the rest, 13 per cent went to direct grant schools and 19 per cent to other state schools, which we can assume were almost all grammar schools. By 1958–9, twenty years later, independent schools were down to 53 per cent, direct grants up to 15 per cent and state schools up to 30 per cent. By 1964–5, independents were down again to 45 per cent, direct grants up to 17 per cent and state schools up to 34 per cent. But this was an accelerating process. The following year – the last recorded by Franks and the latest I have been able to obtain – independents were down to 41 per cent, direct grants still at 17 per cent and state schools up to 40 per cent.

(These totals do not add up to 100 per cent because of the inclusion of 'others' presumably educated at home or in foreign countries.) I have been unable to verify a statement made by Michael Beloff, a former President of Trinity College, Oxford, that the state schools were winning 70 per cent of Oxford places by the early 1970s – though this seems perfectly possible based on the earlier figures. The widespread introduction of comprehensives after October 1965 would not have begun to drag this figure down until the mid-1970s, because so many schools kept their grammar streams until the last pre-comprehensive pupils had completed their A levels.

If direct grant schools and state schools are counted together, the non-private sector was taking the majority of places at Oxford by the mid-1960s, without any special measures or favours and despite entrance exams which – as Franks noted – greatly favoured the traditional public schools. Had things continued in this way, it seems likely that the private sector, already in trouble, would have been severely eclipsed by schools based upon merit – without any lowering of educational standards. As it is, both the ancient universities now give roughly half their places to pupils from private schools, which educate about 7 per cent of pupils, because they would be mad not do so. These schools provide students who are best qualified to benefit from their courses. A high proportion of the state school students come from the small number of remaining grammar schools, now far more exclusive than in the 1960s because of tremendous competition for each place, and far more middle class because middle-class parents pay high premiums to live in the catchment areas of such schools, and send their children to expensive preparatory schools to help them pass the entrance examinations. The other Oxford and Cambridge state entrants come mainly from privileged 'comprehensives' in wealthy areas, where access is controlled by the price of houses, or from other secretly selective schools, mainly but not always religious foundations.

For faith is not the only cover under which such things can be achieved. An example of another form of secret state school privilege was provided by the anti-selection Labour politician Lord Hattersley, who (*The Guardian*, 22 February 2005) visited the Thomas Telford School, in a Shropshire new town, often held up by advocates of comprehensives as an example of the idea working in practice. Hattersley decided that the school, which officially describes itself as 'comprehensive' in its prospectus is in fact 'too good to be true' with its extraordinary examination results and its tiny truancy problem. Its take-up of free school meals, the best measure of poverty among parents, is half the national average. And it has far fewer 'special needs' pupils than any other school in the area.

Hattersley concluded: 'Thomas Telford's success is largely attributable to its admissions policy.' He noted: 'The first stage of the admissions procedure, the application, is itself selection. By requiring parents and guardians to initiate the process, the school automatically limits the list of prospective pupils to children from families that have enough interest and self-confidence to try for something out of the ordinary.'

But what follows is even more striking, for anyone who believes that selection has been abolished in most of Britain. You have to pay close attention here – as cunning and well-informed local parents no doubt do. Hattersley describes the process. 'Selection of one sort or another is unavoidable in a school that does not base admissions on the proximity of the applicant's home.' His implication, that proximity cannot itself be selective, is typical of his refusal to recognise the single most pernicious form of educational privilege in the country, but he has to be given credit for his clear analysis of one of the other methods by which it operates. He continues:

There are 1,234 applicants for 168 places in September – 36 from the 'lowest ability band', 109 from the 'highest'. The National Foundation for Educational Research banding scheme allows only seven to be enrolled from each of those two groups. So a cull is necessary.

When Thomas Telford was first opened, candidates for admission were interviewed by the head. The practice was abandoned because of the storm of protest it caused. Now parents must 'provide a copy of their child's year 5 report from the present school and details of a child's attendance'. They also complete an application form. This year's 'application for admission' includes a series of class-loaded questions, concerning the availability of a 'quiet place to study' and the occupations of parents. It wants to know about 'any outstanding sporting, musical or other activities'.

Lord Hattersley is quite right to be suspicious of this, though no doubt his response would be to stop it from happening altogether – for reasons to be discussed below. While this system is obviously selective, it is far more unfair than the eleven-plus exam which used to decide these matters in the days of grammar schools. Precisely because the procedures are coded and semi-secret, designed not to attract too much attention or look too much like selection, only the smarter parents will understand them and fight their way through them. The old eleven-plus was, by contrast, open to all and did not require pushy or informed parents to ensure a reasonable chance for a clever boy or girl whose mother and father had poor schooling and no knowledge or understanding of the education system. The new arrangements, by contrast, actively favour those who already have privileges and so work against those without them. The extent of this problem was made clear in September 2005 when ConfED, representing local education authority leaders, called for regulations to stop some state schools covertly selecting well-off children by interview, in the hope that this policy will help their standing in exam league tables. It is this secret, underhand and unregulated selection by class and wealth which lies behind much of the recent division in the Labour Party over Ruth Kelly's Education Act, though it is interesting that the rebels are silent about selection by house price. The sordid arrangement we now have is the worst of all possible worlds

Unfair, secret selection has grown as open, public, fair selection has been stifled. The abolition, soon after 1997, of the Assisted Places Scheme destroyed the last remaining official escape route for bright youngsters from poor homes. The scheme, undoubtedly abused by some middle-class parents, more or less replaced the entirely fair direct grant system. The direct grant system, which was far less open to abuse than Assisted Places, had paid certain private schools directly to offer a large number of places to clever children (selected by examination) from homes which could not afford fees, so opening many excellent independent day schools to the children of the poor. Labour politicians nowadays frequently call for the independent sector to share its facilities with state schools. Yet their party abolished direct grant schools which actually did this in a way that benefited the children of many Labour voters.

Labour did this soon after its main attack on the grammar schools was complete. By doing so they showed that it was not unfairness or abuse they objected to, but the very idea that private schools should take subsidised pupils from the state sector. The inferior Assisted Places Scheme was introduced on their return to power by a Tory Party always unwilling to turn back any clocks. Instead of creating places open to competitive entry through a block grant, it paid the fees individually. Despite the abuses of the scheme there were also many silent successes. An assisted place, to my own personal knowledge, certainly enabled one bright child from a poor home in Jarrow to attend the superb Newcastle Royal Grammar School for Boys, thus transforming his life out of all recognition. I met this child, and several like him, and have no doubt that the scheme's faults were wiped out by the great benefits these young people received at its hands. It is, once more, painful to imagine many other such children with the doors of opportunity slammed hard in their faces by this measure.

Now we come to the curious part of this business. You might think, from the passion and money spent on creating a comprehensive school system, that there had been some research from somewhere that showed that it would provide a better education system than the one that had existed before. Since the abolition of selection, direct grants and Assisted Places has undeniably destroyed access to good schools for poor families, the comprehensive revolution must presumably have been known to be likely to provide a generally better education to all. There is no such research. Better education was not and is not the purpose of comprehensive schools. So what was it?

There is no doubt that the idea was popular, or at least acceptable, among many to begin with. The Tory Party's attempts to save selection were usually feeble, because its leaders feared the wrath of middle-class voters whose children were failing the eleven-plus. This is proof, if you like, that the exam was finding working-class talent in the primary schools. The arrangements were also needlessly unfair, with some areas far more endowed with grammar schools than others. The 1965 figures are in some ways surprising. A child in Merthyr Tydfil had a 40 per cent chance of going to grammar school. A child in Ipswich had only a 12 per cent chance. In the county boroughs of England – then the major towns and cities which governed their own schools – the chances ranged from a miserable 8 per cent to a reasonable 34 per cent. In the English counties, the range varied from 13 per cent to 29 per cent. Yet 66 per cent of parents, surveyed by the Campaign for the Advancement of State Education, wanted a grammar school education for their children. Agreeing to a comprehensive system because there were not enough grammar schools was an extraordinarily thoughtless response to an undoubted problem. Would it not have been easier to create new grammar schools in areas where they were lacking? Yet it is typical of the general Tory reaction to radicalism, when that radicalism becomes popular. They always prefer panic and retreat to a proper examination of the issue. They never try to understand the motives of their opponents. There is no doubt that the old selective system could be harsh and unfair. There were far too few grammar schools, especially in the industrial areas. Those that existed discriminated against girls, wrongfully and wastefully. Children only had one chance, though the original 1943 education White Paper had promised that this would not be so.

The secondary moderns were often not very good schools, though there is evidence that some were academically successful and by the end some were even sending pupils to university. In 1961 more than 1,440 secondary modern schools (out of 3,800) entered 31,000 pupils for GCE exams, of which 810 took exams at A level. The technical schools originally promised had mostly never been built.

But it is also undeniable that the grammar schools were performing well. British public life, artistic, academic, literary, political, journalistic, is populated with the brilliant products of a system that, movingly, lifted many thousands of boys and girls into lives their parents could never have imagined. Of all the post-war dreams of improvement and opportunity, it was the one that came nearest to coming true, and the one which did the most to destroy the indefensible silly snobberies and prejudices of pre-war Britain. You might have thought that those who hate unfairness would have loved such a system and tried to widen it. They might have called for the building of more grammar schools. They might have adopted the German system that selected (and still selects) by assessment and agreement between parents and teachers. They might have offered a second chance to transfer at thirteen. They might have put one-tenth of the effort into improving the secondary moderns that they would later put into creating and building huge new comprehensives. They might have created the missing technical schools that this country still needs so badly. They did none of these things. It is all sadly like the famous story of Randolph Churchill's operation, for the removal of a tumour that turned out to be non-malignant. Evelyn Waugh, on hearing this news, mischievously said it was typical of the medical profession that they should have rummaged throughout Randolph's entire body to find the one thing that was not malignant and then removed it. The educational reformers found the one part of the British state school system that was performing well, and they smashed it up with the vigour and zeal usually shown by madmen, drunks or fanatics. It ranks as the most extraordinary episode of institutional destruction since the Dissolution of the Monasteries. Its supporters were neither mad nor drunk. They were entirely rational. But they were fanatics. Those who have puzzled over Anthony Crosland's furious, bitter assertion that he would close down 'every ****ing grammar school in England' – that a civilised and educated person should have spoken in this coarse and savage fashion – should consider that there might in fact be a rational explanation for Crosland's rage, but that it will not be pleasant to hear.

The mystery is easily explained. The comprehensive project was from the very start a political one, not an educational one. This is why the selection by catchment area, selection by faith or camouflaged selection by subtle class bias, all of which look like crude dodges to most people, are acceptable to those who use them. Examined with cold reason, it is most unfair that well-off people such as these should obtain scarce places in good state schools by use of wealth or cunning. By doing so, they deprive poor families of those places. If they were genuinely concerned for the underprivileged, they would pay private school fees and create more room for the needy in schools such as the Oratory and Camden Girls. But this ideology has nothing to do with practical charity or genuine consideration for the poor. It is about the worship of an abstract idea. The first most important thing is that the school to which the Left elite send their children is state-controlled, that is *not private*. The second most important is that it can be described as a comprehensive school even though its entry is not in fact truly comprehensive. Mrs Cherie Blair once employed solicitors to write me an unpleasant letter after I implied in a newspaper article about the Blairs' personal education policy, and its contrast with their official one, that the London Oratory was not a comprehensive school. The dispute was resolved after I wrote in the same newspaper that it was indeed a comprehensive, in the same way that Number Ten Downing Street is an inner-city terraced house.

For the Blairs, and the rest of them, the moral question is an ideological one. It is not what you do that matters, it is the opinion your action endorses. If state schools existed with Quelch-type teachers in mortar boards, house prefects, fagging, real tennis courts and cricket teams, the socialist elite would probably send their children to them – provided that they were officially comprehensive and that there was no nonsense about Christianity. Of course, proper comprehensive schools cannot actually be like this, though it is surprising how many of the characteristics of such schools have been quietly preserved or revived within an allegedly comprehensive system – even including single-sex establishments.

Rich and powerful Leftists know perfectly well what makes a good education for their own young, just like the elite Moscow parents, KGB officers, party apparatchiks and Central Committee members who in Soviet days used every ounce of influence to get their young into Secondary School Number One in Moscow. I know one product of this school whose incorruptible grandfather, a stern former Red Army general and medal-hung veteran of the Great Patriotic War, abandoned his Bolshevik principles for the only time in his life to secure her entry to this first-rate establishment. A similar system was still operating, in 2008, at the Lenin High School in Havana, notorious in Cuba for favouring the children of the Castro-supporting elite. North Korea has a comparable arrangement involving the Mangyongdae Revolutionary School in Pyongyang.

In our incurious world, surprisingly few people know who invented comprehensive schools or the expression 'comprehensive school'. The name of Sir Graham Savage

(1886–1981), one of the most influential reformers of the
twentieth century, is wrongly forgotten. Who was he? He
seems to have been one of those very bright middle-class
Victorian children who won his way to Cambridge by sheer
talent, a product of an ancient grammar school in Norwich
rather than any of the great public schools. After Cambridge,
he became a teacher, but an unusual one who taught in
Canada and Egypt, living for a while in an Egyptian village
to learn colloquial Arabic. World War I took him to both
Gallipoli and France. He briefly taught at Eton before
becoming a civil servant. Pictures of him later in life show a
genial, bald, bespectacled old gentleman rather like Arthur
Ransome, in a waistcoat, a watch-chain and a walrus
moustache, his face disfigured by the deep scar caused by an
honourable war wound.

He is a reassuring figure, avuncular and kindly in
appearance. But as a young civil servant he originated a plan
that would change Britain beyond recognition. On behalf of
what was then called the Board of Education he made a three-
month visit to North America to study the school systems of
Ontario, New York State and Indiana. This visit led to Board
of Education pamphlet number 56, published in 1928. In it,
Savage said he had been impressed by a non-selective system
with no hurdle at the age of eleven. In an interview with *The
Times* many years later (2 April 1965), he made it clear – too
late – how many reservations he had also had. He was shocked
by the gargantuan size of the non-selective high schools, built
on a scale then unknown in the British Isles. He concluded that
between the ages of six and fourteen, two years of schooling
were lost, by comparison with the English selective system. He
had observed at the time that in the 'junior high' schools the
'pupil with intellectual interests is held back to a predetermined
rate of travel. If he is a musician, or has artistic talent, or
proposes to be an electrician or any other kind of craftsman,
he gets a special course of work which will help him to reach
his goal.' However:

if he is merely a mathematician or has linguistic powers he must travel with the rest until, having reached the ninth grade (aged 14), he is able to begin the ordinary syllabus of the senior school. The type with high intellectual interests is the only one that is not encouraged to develop its abilities.

He also warned 'Democracy, in America at least, is too often interpreted as meaning that everyone shall have the same treatment. The writer likes to believe that a truer conception is that each should be allowed to develop himself to his fullest extent as long as he interferes with no-one else.'

As for the 'senior high' schools, which took pupils from fourteen to eighteen:

the interests of the pupils who will not stay the whole course were well looked after, but something is certainly lost by the ablest. The very definite effort made to relate abstract conceptions or simple scientific ideas to practical life may be necessary for the very dull, but it deprives the abler pupil of the delight and exhilaration which comes when he is allowed to make the discovery of the relationship spontaneously. It shows a lack of faith in the value of purely intellectual effort.

His obituary noted that after his retirement, he:

seemed to voice some misgiving about comprehensive education. His respect for intellect and academic excellence appeared to make him apprehensive for the future of grammar schools, which, he felt, were a precious part of English education. It is very doubtful if the disappearance of long established grammar schools into larger units would have given him any joy.

Despite expressing so many doubts, Savage continued to act throughout his professional life as if he believed that the

American system was preferable to the English one. He was the man chosen by the Labour radicals of the London County Council to devise the first scheme for comprehensive schools in Britain after World War II. These enthusiasts were not – at that time – completely typical of Labour opinion. The first Education Minister in the 1945 Labour government, the legendary Jarrow Left-winger Ellen Wilkinson, enforced and defended the division between grammar and secondary modern schools. So did her successor George Tomlinson, though the Left-dominated Labour Party conference urged 'the 'rapid development' of 'common secondary schools' in 1948 (David Kynaston, *A World to Build*, Bloomsbury, London, 2008 p. 221). Certainly the Left had for some time been hoping to use education to pursue equality. The National Association of Labour Teachers had for years been campaigning for what it called 'multilateral' schools. The radical London Labour Party was filled with a glowing idealism on the subject. This utopianism was typified by Margaret (Postgate) Cole in her pamphlet *What is a Comprehensive School?* from those times. The pamphlet bears on its cover an idealised picture of the planned Kidbrooke Comprehensive, all white concrete and sweeping lawns, like a propaganda tract from the German Democratic Republic (another enthusiastic supporter of comprehensive schooling, replaced by new grammar schools by popular demand soon after liberty returned to its territory in 1989). The prose within is similarly millenialistic. Miss Cole writes that 'While the [1944 Education] Act was still in the making, the Labour London County Council made up its mind that all London children should have the right to go to any County school *of their choice* [my italics] without any question of test or examination.' She quotes R. McKinnon Wood, chairman of the LCC Education Committee, as saying that 'the Tories fight this great democratic plan for secondary education by all possible means'. She also quotes Tory opponents of the scheme as claiming that the result would be free mediocrity for all, that such a school would be a 'mass factory of so-called education' and 'the clever child's progress will be held up by the gropings of the sub-educated'.

The Tories were not the only defenders of the grammar schools. As Stephen Pollard pointed out in the pamphlet the Fabian Society refused to publish:

> The old and successful notion of the grammar school ... was enthusiastically adopted by Fabian socialists such as Sidney Webb and, later, R.H. Tawney, who saw grammar schools (which the 1944 Education Act forced to select on the basis of ability rather social class) as the apotheosis of a socialist meritocracy – opening up opportunities to all on the basis of ability rather than parental wealth.

Pollard blames the change in Labour's position on 'the new post-war Croslandite, Left view' which 'saw social engineering as being more important'. He says Crosland had argued that schooling should be seen as 'a serious alternative to nationalisation in promoting a more just and efficient society'. Though there others who believe – and apparently still believe – that forcing higher-achieving children to share classes with lower achievers will benefit the laggards without hurting the high-flyers, there has yet to be any evidence that this works (see the remarks of Robert Crampton, quoted above, which strongly undermine the idea). What is more, Crosland himself had little idea of what he was really unleashing, any more than Margaret Cole had done when she claimed that a 'grammar school education' would be fully provided within her London comprehensives for those who needed it, or that single-sex education and small schools would survive. Labour's 1964 manifesto, which was the democratic mandate for the destruction of grammar schools, likewise pretended that the new system would extend, not end, grammar school education. It said, in an exceptionally misleading passage:

Labour will get rid of the segregation of children into separate schools caused by 11-plus selection: secondary education will be reorganised on comprehensive lines. Within the new system, grammar school education will be extended: in future no child will he denied the opportunity of benefiting from it through arbitrary selection at the age of 11.

It may be that the authors of this falsehood genuinely believed it. Crosland wrote in *The Future of Socialism* (Jonathan Cape, London, 1956, p. 271) that:

many people still object to the idea of comprehensive schools, not necessarily on grounds of principle, but simply because they fear the results may be bad in practice. The most common fears are, generally, that standards will be lowered, and the clever child held back to the pace of the average child: and specifically that if the school is to cater adequately for advanced and sixth-form study, it must be vast in size.

Noting that at the time of writing (1956) there were then only fourteen comprehensive schools in existence, Crosland says 'there is naturally no conclusive evidence. But a careful study of the experiments to date affords at least preliminary evidence, and this does not bear out the fears expressed. There is no sign of any levelling-down of standards, and some evidence even of the reverse' (ibid).

He adds, crucially:

The main reason is the comprehensive schools have not, as many feared (and some hoped) that they would, mixed children of different abilities in the same class, but have adopted a *system of testing and differentiation designed to produce homogeneous classes of more or less similar standards of more or less similar standards of attainment.* [My italics.]

In other words, the original comprehensives effectively retained selection within the school, and recognised that it was necessary, which was why Crosland was willing to support them. He was quite specific about this, and realised its implications.

> This has shocked some comprehensive enthusiasts, who had hoped for a system of 'social promotion' on the American model, with virtually no grading by ability. But both common sense and American experience suggest that this would lead to a really serious levelling-down of standards, and a quite excessive handicap to the clever child. Division into streams, according to ability, remains essential.

Crosland's heresy continues. He says:

> the object of having comprehensive schools is not to abolish all competition and all envy, which might be rather a hopeless task, but to avoid the extreme social division caused by physical segregation into schools of widely divergent status, and the extreme social resentment caused by failure to win a grammar (or, in future, public) school place, when this is thought to be the only avenue to a 'middle-class' occupation.

But perhaps the most striking part of the argument comes in Crosland's dismissal of the case against comprehensive schools, mainly advanced by those who feared they would suffer from all the ills of the American high schools they were based on:

> Much of the argument against comprehensive schools proceeds by analogy. The critics point to the low standards characteristic of many American high schools. *These low standards are not in dispute* [my italics]. But there are many possible explanations besides the comprehensive character of these schools: for example, the anti-highbrow

and anti-academic ('anti-egghead') tradition of American life, the acute shortage of teachers (especially male teachers) the low quality of many of the teachers (amounting sometimes almost to illiteracy), the insistence on automatic 'social promotion' by age groups, an excessive attachment to Deweyism and 'life-adjustment' education at the expense of more basic academic disciplines, the overwhelming preference for vocational courses, and so on. All or any of these influences, none of which are or need be reproduced in English comprehensive schools, may be responsible for the lower standards.

The critics were, as they so often are, absolutely right. Crosland's reassurances were, as the soothings of progressives so often are, completely wrong. The differences between state schools, all but a few supposedly the same, are vast and are based upon class and wealth as never before. An 'anti-egghead' culture has developed in many schools, with diligent students often derisively mocked as 'boffins', and bullied for being outstanding. A great deal of comprehensive school teaching (though less than at one stage) is in mixed-ability classes. Streaming is virtually unknown, while some setting happens in a minority of schools. The comprehensive experiment also had the ill luck to be introduced at a time of major social and cultural change, which it helped to extend and intensify. The 1964–70 Labour government greatly widened the recruitment of teachers, and changed the way in which they were trained. Many of the new generation of post-1968 students went into teaching, where the spirit of 1968 was continued by other means. Many were not as well educated as those they replaced. Their politics and social attitudes were more radical. Recruitment advertising for state school teachers used, as late as the end of the 1970s, to be concentrated in the conservative *Daily Telegraph*. It is a telling sign of the social revolution in the profession that within twenty years it was mainly concentrated in the Leftish *Guardian*.

The early attempts by comprehensives to mimic grammar-school formality quickly faded away, partly because of the general social revolution, partly because the comprehensive rejection of selection made it difficult, partly because the sheer size of the new schools (a point not often enough realised) made it hard for anyone to control them. Yet there was a lengthy transitional period where many new comprehensives, especially those fashioned from former grammar schools, appeared to fulfil Anthony Crosland's predictions. Changes in the nature of both pupils and teachers would bring this to an end.

The initial experiment in a radical new type of schooling – co-educational, non-academic, informal, without corporal punishment – was at the once-notorious Risinghill School in Islington, under the headship of Michael Duane. Risinghill was closed after much recrimination, and many attacks from conservative newspapers, and also eulogised by Leila Berg in a 1968 book (*Risinghill – Death of a Comprehensive School*, Pelican, London). It turned out to have been the prototype for much of what would follow, but to have been a little too early, and too much all at once, for the state of public opinion. The 1968 generation, who went into teaching in their tens of thousands during the 1970s, were greatly influential in overthrowing the ethos, authority and manners of authoritarian education, and in making many more schools resemble Risinghill much more than they resembled the old grammar schools. No doubt – as so often – their intentions were as noble as Michael Duane's. Yet it is difficult to see that the result has been beneficial for the children of the poor, whom Duane hoped to rescue from misery and hopelessness.

Other schools, even if they stood aside from the comprehensive revolution, have all been affected by the change. Examinations, especially after the reforms of the Thatcher era, are designed to test a 'comprehensive idea' of what education should be, rather than the more rigorous knowledge-based aims of the grammar schools. Even the remaining grammar schools are pressed to conform to the Comprehensive agenda, as are the private schools. They fear punishment and the withdrawal of their valuable charitable status (now under severe examination from a newly militant Charity Commission) if they rebel against the new standards. They were slow to resort to separate or different examinations – though the dissatisfaction with the GCSE and reformed A levels led during 2007 to a much wider adoption of 'International' GCSEs (similar to the old O levels) and the introduction of a 'pre-university' examination by Cambridge University to replace the now much-diluted A levels. Several leading schools also began to take the International Baccalaureate, whose standards are beyond the control of British agencies.

The slowness of the private schools to abandon the official exams has another rather disgraceful reason. In many cases they gain commercial advantage because this dilution of quality allows them to score very high positions in 'league tables' of exam success. These tables, like the exams that define them, do not reward excellence, but do reward close adherence to the norm of drilling and assessment. One of the few schools which deviate from the comprehensive style, Winchester, regularly appears among the poorest performing schools at GCSE when the results for its county (Hampshire) are published. This is obviously a false result, but nobody in politics or mainstream educational journalism ever comments on the anomaly – because it subverts the widespread fantasy that the tables give a true measure of excellence. To deny this would undermine many of the independent schools as well as the entire state system.

Deweyism, or child-centred 'discovery' education is now as much an orthodoxy in Britain as it was in the USA when Crosland wrote *The Future of Socialism*. It is one of the great paradoxes of the Cold War that egalitarianism arrived in Britain in its American form, while this country was officially fighting the egalitarian tyranny of the Soviet Union as the principal ally of the USA. Britain actually became an egalitarian society in the most intense years of the Cold War.

While the great moral and political conflicts seemed to be taking place in Vietnam, Czechoslovakia, Afghanistan and Poland, they were also happening in thousands of school classrooms. And, while the dictatorially egalitarian Soviet project was utterly defeated in global confrontation, a more or less egalitarian ideology was victorious by stealth in one of the principal fortresses of anti-Soviet resistance. The idea that boys and girls could improve their own lives by becoming middle class in increasing numbers, embodied in the grammar school experiment of 1944 to 1965, was supplanted by a quite different idea – that the lives of all could be improved by creating a classless society.

Many conservatives still cannot cope with this knowledge, any more than they can grapple with the equally inconvenient fact that the brand of revolutionary thought known as political correctness began and still flourishes greatly in the supposedly 'Right-wing' USA. It is far easier to make heroic gestures abroad, or defiant speeches damning an unseen or distant enemy than it is to confront and defeat real, dogged foes at home. This helps to explain the lack of a serious Tory opposition to the comprehensive scheme. To condemn comprehensive schools outright would be to defy the dogma of egalitarianism, which Tories have never fought against with any conviction, and which they often appear to support without any idea of what it means. The Conservative Prime Minister from 1990 to 1997, John Major, was fond of declaring his support for a 'classless society'. Equality of outcome, the socialist desire, is increasingly accepted among mainstream thinkers as a desirable aim. As in so many things, there is no longer any debate between the political parties about issues which have divided thinkers down the ages, and divide the population even now.

It would have been quite easy for serious conservatives to fight comprehensive education from the beginning. The response to the Left's campaign was well-made by such figures as Eric James, High Master of Manchester Grammar School. Serious conservatives could also have offered the most rational answer to critics who claimed that selection deprived too many people of a good education. They could have pledged to create large numbers of new grammar schools in areas where they were sparse, so ending much of this waste. They could have made a serious effort to create the technical schools which are still so badly needed. It was always going to be difficult to find a good purpose for the secondary modern schools, and many of these could have been replaced by greater numbers of grammars, or supplanted by technical secondaries. But, lacking any coherent idea of what they wished to defend, the Tory Party nationally chose to let matters drift until the Left's case was broadly accepted. They even allowed state schools to reach the stage where middle-class parents could be persuaded to favour comprehensive schools because their own children might fail the eleven-plus. It has been argued that this was a conscious movement among the better-off, who anticipated that comprehensives, selecting through catchment areas, would in future favour the middle class, who would have exclusive access to the better schools. This would certainly prove to be the case, though at a very high cost in the general standard of state schooling. But it is hard to believe that many really foresaw this unintended consequence of the Crosland Revolution.

As in so many other areas of policy and action, the Tories persuaded themselves that this decisive battle for the national soul was not in fact important at all. It was easy for them to do this, for most Tory politicians have neither knowledge nor personal experience of the state education system as it affects most people. They either benefit from elite state schools in sheltered and exceptional catchment areas, or they pay school fees. Rather than engage the enemy on this ground, they repeatedly plan and fight the battles of a previous war, while their radical enemies dash past them on either side, laughing. They cannot grasp that British radicalism took a completely different turn in the 1960s, and that the issues of nationali-sation and Trade Union power are quite dead. For if they did understand this, then they would have to realise just how limited the triumphs of Margaret Thatcher were. They would also have to recognise the extent of their own defeat, and they would have to fight real, difficult and courageous battles to undo the damage.

Labour's real 'Clause Four' is not some obsolete scripture about the means of production, distribution and exchange. It is its unalterable opposition to school selection on the grounds of ability – a more or less insane ideological position applied to no other field of human endeavour and yet now written into the law of England and endorsed by the Conservative front bench into the bargain.

But they are not the only ones trapped in an unthinking obsession with the past. It may be so – and I suspect it is – that a small group of radicals really does seek to use the schools for a revolutionary egalitarian transformation of Britain. It may be that they see the lowered standards, bullying and truancy as a price worth paying for this aim, and that they will only become interested in rigour and discipline once their long march is over. This is a habit of revolutions, which attack every social norm and source of order until their enemies are destroyed, and then turn furiously on their own radicals, imposing a very orderly new order. The British cultural revolution, however, has been dragging on so long and is still so inconclusive that the reactionary moment is a long way off.

There is interesting but fleeting evidence of the existence of a new educational establishment which prefers to keep its debates private. According to the *Sunday Telegraph* of 27 June 1993, this faction is called the All Souls Group, and it holds its 'clandestine thrice-yearly meetings' in an oak-panelled room at Oxford University. No minutes are kept of the meetings, and no papers or public statements ever emerge. The discussions are protected by Chatham House Rules, which ensure that proceedings are off the record. Such people would never have won an election if they had said openly that they were going to do what they did (as we have seen, the plan for national comprehensive education was significantly misrepresented in the 1964 Labour manifesto). Their utopianism has little in common with the realistic equality of opportunity once sought by the serious Labour movement whose party they now control. It is important to remember that before 1950 Labour supported grammar schools, that they most definitely did benefit large numbers of poor homes and that there are even now serious voices in Labour who see the case for selection. It is worth mentioning here that in the former West Germany, it was mass protests by parents which successfully stopped a plan to abolish selection in Social Democratic North-Rhine Westphalia, and that popular pressure in the former East Germany, where socialism remains the strongest political force, has insisted on the creation of new grammar schools to replace the comprehensive *Gesamtschule* system adopted by the Workers' and Peasants' State. Handsome new grammar schools (*Gymnasien*) are to be seen in many towns and cities in the old East Germany.

It is certainly true that the English selective system had many faults forty years ago. Many of the criticisms of it from the Left were quite justified. It plainly needed serious reform and change. It would be absurd to deny it, and – to have this debate seriously – both sides must grasp that the argument is not about returning to an unchanged pre-Crosland landscape. But the introduction of comprehensive education cured none of those faults. It made them worse, at great cost. A 2005 London School of Economics report showed that social mobility in Britain had actually declined during the period following the abolition of academic selection. It phrased its conclusions delicately: 'The strength of the relationship between educational attainment and family income, especially for access to higher education, is at the heart of Britain's low mobility culture and what sets us apart from other European and North American countries.' In other words, since the grammar schools were abolished, family wealth, and nothing else, has decided what sort of education a child receives.

The egalitarians fiercely refuse to admit it. Their determination to deny that their experiment has failed is one of the reasons for the curious annual festival of lies which accompanies the issuing of examination results. These purport to show an ever-expanding level of knowledge among the products of egalitarian schools. Rather than admit that standards have fallen, the egalitarians have changed the standards. John Marks (in *The Betrayed Generation – Standards in British Schools 1950–2000*, Centre for Policy Studies, London, 2001) argues that the general lowering of standards and rigour since the end of selection is one of the main reasons behind the current drive to devalue examinations. This debasing of the currency of knowledge certainly might have been designed to conceal the depth and length and breadth and height of the failure of comprehensive schools. It might well have done so if a number of informed critics had not kept up a steady bombardment casting doubt on official claims of constant improvement.

This devaluation damages the nation as a whole and everyone in it, limiting access not only to high culture but to the basic amenities of literacy, destroying national fellow-feeling by dimming knowledge of shared history, cutting us off from much of the world by failure to teach foreign languages, damaging our inventive powers by leaving many children utterly ignorant of the hard sciences. There is no serious dispute among the intelligent and the informed that this is taking place. There are two pieces of indisputable evidence of falling standards: in 2000 the Engineering Council published the results of a ten-year survey into the maths skills of university students starting maths, science and engineering courses. Identical tests were given to comparable groups of students each year. They found that, though A-level grades improved, skills declined. For example, students who failed their A-levels in 1991 had better test results than those who scored C grades in 1998. Meanwhile, Durham University had been giving an unvarying general ability test to students since 1988. By 2003, they found that students of the same ability were getting two A-level grades higher than they were fifteen years before. In a study published in June 2006, Durham University confirmed a long-term inflation in A-level grades, varying from subject to subject but detectable in all of them.

The question which arises is why the educated, conscious servants of the state should seek to pretend that educational standards are rising when the opposite is true. The answer is that they have put equality before education, wish to continue to do so, and therefore seek to hide from themselves as well as from others the terrible collateral damage caused by their war against privilege. As in that other great idealistic enterprise of the dogmatic Left, the invasion of Iraq, the broken eggs lie scattered about everywhere, but there is no omelette to be seen. Even on its own terms, the thing is a failure, and worse than a failure. Can any good, kind, reasonable person approve of this destruction of hope, or of these lies? Would the Fabians of 1910, or the Labour Cabinet of 1945, or even the Labour leadership of 1964, or even Anthony Crosland or Sir Graham Savage, now approve of the consequences of what they did, especially for the poor they claimed to be helping? This is not the case with the Conservatives, who might have unpleasant but logical reasons for smashing the grammar schools. A cynical class-war Tory might say (provided he thought nobody was listening) that comprehensive education had first saved and then greatly reinforced private schooling; he or she might add that it had re-established privileges threatened by the 1945 social revolution. He might say that it had closed the better state schools to everyone but the well-off middle class, and he might exult over that. But how can Labour, a movement which has always claimed to speak and act for the poor, continue to pursue a policy which, year by year, destroys the hopes of millions of poor children?

12

'The age of the train'

Imagine a government that behaves like this: First, it commissions a well-known businessman to prepare a report on the profitability of the road network. Second, the businessman, famed for his 'tough' and 'no-nonsense' approach to sentimentalists, produces the expected ruthless document, which shows that the great majority of suburban streets, secondary roads and country lanes have absolutely no economic justification and cost far more to maintain than they can be said to contribute to the economy of the country. About 20 per cent of the roads carry about 80 per cent of the traffic. Only a central core of motorways and trunk routes can actually justify their enormous cost in the straightforward accounting terms on which the issue has to be judged. Finally, dismissing the protests of millions as silly nostalgia and 'Not-in-my-backyard' selfishness, the government withdraws the mountainous state subsidy which pays to keep these roads open. Then, fearing that it may lose the next election to a party which does not share its virulent anti-road prejudice, it sends out diggers to plough up the condemned highways, blow up bridges and generally make its actions irreversible. It even hastens the sale of land along the former road routes, in the hope that houses and offices will be swiftly built where those roads once ran. Later, when the closure of the 'uneconomic' routes results in very heavy use of some of the remaining roads, it introduces increasingly heavy tolls to drive users away and on to other forms of transport, rather than expanding them.

We once had such a government. In many ways we still do. But its lunatic hostility was – and continues to be – directed against the railway network, rather than the roads. It has managed to destroy one of the most precious pieces of British social and economic capital. Sizeable towns such as Abingdon, Witney, Cirencester, Tavistock, Gosport, Mansfield, Hawick and Ripon lost all railway connections (some have since been restored but many have not). The only major East–West railway line in the country, linking three of the main trunk routes at points well north of London, was shut (the equivalent, in many ways, of closing the northern section of the M25). Many other places lost rational, direct rail links with their neighbours and their hinterland. The country's only line capable of carrying continental freight wagons from the Channel to the North was pulled up and left to the weeds. The only civilised transport connection between the university cities of Oxford and Cambridge was destroyed. A costly and beautifully engineered express line between Exeter and Plymouth was torn from its sleepers, leaving the West Country with only one rail connection to the capital even though that line became heavily congested each summer, and was vulnerable to storm damage each winter where it ran along the coast. Dozens of two-track lines were reduced to single tracks, a certain recipe for delay and decline. Country districts, once served by regular trains, were left to the mercy of fickle bus companies. A means of transport invented and perfected in this country and ideally suited to its landscape was relegated, ever afterwards, to a secondary position and made to feel ashamed of not paying for itself, whereas roads and motor cars (and airlines) were powerfully and increasingly subsidised from tax revenue, or by exemption from tax, without any political pressure for them to reduce their costs. From the moment these changes took place, a private motor car rapidly became the only practical way of making most journeys across the country. And a motor lorry became the only practical way of transferring freight.

The process did not end there. The practicality of the car for longer journeys quickly meant that many more households acquired cars, which they found were also cheap and easy to use for shorter journeys. This had two further effects. The number of cars on the roads slowed down bus services and made life less pleasant for walkers and bicyclists, who faced growing danger, noise and aggressive competition for limited space. Inevitably, this increased the use of, and the demand for cars. It also stimulated democratic political pressure for the building of more roads – of two kinds. Fast dual carriageways were needed to cope with the greater numbers of cars. And bypass and ring roads were needed to carry those cars away from residential neighbourhoods. Both these developments once again encouraged cars and discouraged walkers and bicyclists. The faster speeds on the dual carriageways, and their greater width, made them more risky and unpleasant than ordinary roads for non-car users. Anti-personnel fences were built to prevent pedestrians crossing them except at designated places.

Those designated places could no longer be simple zebra crossings, where drivers were obliged to stop if a human being placed her foot upon the road. Instead, pedestrians had to wait, sometimes for as long as a minute, for allegedly 'pedestrian controlled' lights to change and allow them to cross, in a few brief seconds, hurried along by urgent bleepings. Alternatively, they were expected to use dank, ill-lit and inconvenient tunnels, apparently designed for the convenience of robbers and aggressive beggars and approached by long and exasperating ramps or steps. These new fast highways, and bypass roads, tended to be designed wholly for the convenience of drivers. Complex one-way systems became necessary to join them to existing roads. They swung from place to pace using extravagant, land-hungry curves. Non-motorists who dared to use them found themselves compelled to take long ways round – which did not seem long to a motorist in control of a large and powerful engine, but which were wearing and dispiriting for a bicyclist reliant only on his calf muscles. And so every step taken to adapt the country for the driver was also a step to make it more unpleasant, dangerous and inconvenient for the non-drivers – who happened to be a majority of the population.

Those too young to remember the pre-Beeching age (for the ruthless businessman was Dr Richard Beeching, who would eventually be raised to the peerage as a reward for his stupidity) cannot begin to grasp the destructive frenzy which rapidly swept away the condemned lines. For a period of a few years, the traveller would groan to see stark notices, pasted up at his local station, declaring the fast-approaching withdrawal of services. Occasionally, very occasionally, protests saved some lines. But it is thanks to Dr Beeching, for instance, that there is no longer a direct rail route from the North and Midlands through Oxford and Didcot to Southampton (trains must go in and out of Reading, a long eastward detour). Yet, at colossal expense in money and landscape, a direct *road* route has now been built on this route, a road which carries a gigantic tonnage of freight and passenger traffic that might have gone by rail. Thanks to the far greater friction experienced by road traffic (friction between rubber and tarmac is roughly thirty-three times greater than that between steel wheel and steel rail) the road is immensely less efficient than the destroyed railway used to be. Had the existing rail route been upgraded and electrified, which would have cost far less in money and beauty than the building of the much-resisted Newbury bypass alone, who knows what we might have been spared in ugliness, fuel pollution, noise and danger? And who cares? For the people who should in theory have been voicing these criticisms, political Conservatives, have for decades been the loyal propagandists of the 'build more roads' lobby, worshippers of what Margaret Thatcher termed the 'Great Car Economy'.

This chapter does not pretend to be a great exposé of an anti-rail conspiracy. Perhaps there was such a thing. The Tory Minister of Transport at the time of Beeching, the raffish Ernest Marples, held (through his wife) substantial interests in the construction industry while he was a minister, but this was not thought strange or unethical at the time. The construction industry, the motor industry, the oil industry and the land development industry all could have had substantial interests in a major diversion of resources from rail to road. There is far more logic in railways being closed to suit such interests than there ever was in the Beeching report. There have been alleged conspiracies, in such places as Los Angeles, where oil and motor industries are said to have bought up public transport systems only so as to run them down and so create a greater market for their products. Some even view the presidency of Dwight D. Eisenhower as a sort of personal conspiracy against the North American railroads, since it was Eisenhower who signed into law the Bill authorising enormous federal spending on Interstate Highways (the USA's equivalent of motorways).

This rather un-American state subsidy for road travel was excused on the unconvincing grounds that the new roads would be evacuation arteries for the USA's great cities in the event of an atomic war. Eisenhower was said to have been impressed by the way in which Nazi Germany's autobahns survived heavy bombing far better than railways (though this is not borne out by the case of Iraq, where – in my personal experience – the modern and well-built motorway between Baghdad and the Jordanian border was easily and severely damaged by American bombing planes and could plainly have been rendered completely unusable had the US Air Force so chosen). However, the evacuation pretext allowed political conservatives to pretend that it was not a subsidy at all, and to imagine that they had not violated their supposed principles on such matters.

The British decision to build motorways in heavily subsidised competition with the poorly subsidised and truncated railways, which broadly coincided with the state-sponsored sabotage of the British railway system, certainly *looks* like a planned development. No doubt the coincidence theorists have their views on this. But I know of no documents or confessions which would substantiate this claim, so I cannot make it. Perhaps one day we will have such evidence. But until then, my question is this: just as the destruction of grammar schools has hurt the poor, the destruction of railways has hurt tradition, order and beauty, and led to the break-up of communities and the rape of much-loved landscape. It has also destroyed a major export industry and a special skill in which this country was pre-eminent. What is conservative or patriotic about Britain's neglect of railways, and its heavy spending of taxpayers' cash on – and promotion of – major motor highways, in the era since 1955? If you have an objection to state subsidy on principle, as the railway-haters claim to do – then surely it applies just as much to road subsidies as to railway ones?

It is easy to see that these changes benefited certain industries – the quarrying, construction and civil engineering sectors have never ceased to benefit from large government contracts ever since, and now do rather well from the constant need to repair the roads and bridges that have, so often, failed to last anything like as long as they were intended to. The motor industry and the road haulage industry, likewise, were obvious gainers, as was the petroleum sector. If the road boom has benefited some industries, others – notably Britain's once-flourishing railway locomotive sector and carriage works – have practically disappeared. The country that originated the railway now imports most, if not all, of its engines and coaches, as well as specialised equipment for track repair. And hundreds of thousands of jobs, stable, reasonably paid and responsible, have vanished as the railways have contracted.

Most cars and lorries on British roads were British made, in British-owned factories, back in 1955. But virtually none is now. And what are the national benefits of becoming ever more reliant upon imported fuel, which comes from politically unstable and often sordidly despotic parts of the world, and whose price is destined to rise forever, as the great nations of Asia compete with Europe and North America for ever-scarcer deposits?

It also scarcely seems a conservative foreign policy to put our own economic security and prosperity entirely at the mercy of Muslim autocracies, Central Asian dictatorships and now an authoritarian Russia which has shown itself capable of using its oil and gas power to put pressure on client governments.

But the strongest conservative arguments against the feverish desire to build roads and fill them with cars are social and aesthetic. Roads destroy and distort established ways of living. The traditional English town, with its defined centre, ancient street pattern and comfortable shape, was not destroyed by the coming of the railway. It was enhanced. Everything still remained within easy walking distance of everything else, while it was now possible to travel at speed to neighbouring cities or to anywhere in the country.

When the state decided to prefer roads and motor cars, every town and city in the country was rapidly, irrevocably reshaped. The car could not travel at speed unless a bypass or an inner ring road – or both – were built in or around towns of any size. These new roads had to be carved through the old street pattern and only worked if they entirely ignored it. The ugliness and crudity of this effect can be seen in many places. One is at Spon End in Coventry, where a lovely remnant of what might have been rebuilt (but was not) as one of the world's most handsome medieval cities is abruptly sliced off by the course of an inner ring of incredible ugliness and brutality. York (whose medieval centre survives in far better shape) is badly afflicted, as the traffic engineers have driven their geometric highway along the foot of the old city walls. Any sort of organic relationship between the old city and the rest of York is made impossible by this unlovely dry moat of fumes and noise, subsiding only in the dead of night into a bleak, disproportionate circular desert. Birmingham may never have been an urban gem (though George Orwell describes its pre-war Bull Ring, incredibly, as having been similar to Norwich marketplace), but the damage done to its integrity by fast motor roads is irreparable. There is hardly a town or city in all England which has not been wounded or ruined by insensitive and anomalous road construction – which has notably failed to solve the traffic problems it was supposed to ease.

There is another radical, unconservative effect, the atomisation of society. Private cars are seen as a blessing by their users precisely because they separate them from their fellow-creatures. A person living in a modern suburb could quite easily walk the short distance from his front door to his car (parked in what used to be his neighbourly front garden and is now an unfriendly patch of concrete, paving or tarmac) and drive to work, cocooned in steel; then spend the day among the artificial relationships of the workplace; then return home and move straight from his car to his home. During this process he would never see, or speak to, even his immediate neighbour. While in his car, all his activities would be entirely private.

Once again, I cannot think why a social or moral conservative should want to make this happen. Nor can I see why anyone concerned for family and private life should want the widespread dispersal of families which the car and the town planning it encourages have created. Individuals whose main contact with the world outside their home is through television, telephone or radio are unlikely to form the little platoons of private enthusiasm, the clubs and societies that make traditional societies function and keep alive their customs and memory.

There is another element here which makes even less sense. Railways were invented in Britain. Without them we would never have been the great power we became. They shaped our landscape and our cities. They were one of our greatest exports to the rest of the world. Our greatest engineers were concerned in building them and designing their engines. Recognised by everyone who saw them as being more than mere machines, the great express locomotives were symbols of industrial might, just as much as Dreadnought battleships were symbols of naval power. Many of their staff were ex-servicemen obeying a hierarchical discipline not unlike that of the armed forces. It is impossible to believe that a conservative, in his deepest nature a patriot, could scorn or seek to destroy or belittle this of all industries,

Yet the British Conservative Party is correctly identified as the anti-railway party by those both inside and outside it. Margaret Thatcher pointedly seldom travelled by train. It was a Conservative government that asked for the Beeching report and mostly accepted it. It was a Conservative government that decided on a particularly damaging form of privatisation of the railways, despite warnings from every knowledgeable person that it would do harm. One of the very few Conservative MPs who was sympathetic to the railways, Robert Adley, was excused on the grounds of being 'eccentric' rather than recognised as being right when the rest of his party was wrong. The Labour Party, which has a more complicated relationship with the railways, was for years allowed to give the impression of being in favour of them, but it did little to undo Beeching between 1964 and 1970 (actually closing at least one line that Beeching wanted kept open). And it has shown in all its years in office since 1997 that it is in fact no better than the Tories. But why should it be better than them? A socially 'progressive' party will not necessarily favour such a conservative thing. The Trades Union movement had (and still has) many members in industries which compete with the railways and object to their being subsidised. It has no patriotism. It is wedded to the European vision which in fact imposed the privatisation everyone decries as wrong. This is perhaps why it has done nothing to reverse it.

That sort of private sacrifice of an old principle in favour of a new necessity is as easy to explain as a secret Tory hatred of grammar schools. Such a loathing is entirely rational, assuming that the Tory Party is no more than the coarse spokesman of selfishness that its opponents claim it to be. What cannot be justified is the practical destructive hatred shown by an allegedly conservative party for a great conservative institution like the national railway system. It can only be understood as part of a wider understanding – that the Tory Party does not love Britain, any more than the Labour Party loves the poor. Both obey masters quite different from the ones they claim to serve. Neither genuinely speaks for the tribe it is supposed to head. The great divisions of Britain – Roundhead and Cavalier, Norman and Saxon, North and South, are not reflected in our official politics. Nor is the great modern split between those who oppose the domination of the country by the EU, and those who see it as the only safe future. Nor is the most profound disagreement of all, between those who think man is perfectible and those who are sure he is not.

13

A Comfortable Hotel
on the Road to Damascus

In 1997 it would have been impossible to imagine Charles Moore, mannerly Etonian editor of the *Daily Telegraph*, devout Roman Catholic convert and the original 'Young Fogey', joining hands with Nick Cohen, raucous atheistical Left-wing writer for such organs as the *New Statesman* and the *Observer*. Yet less than ten years later they were political allies, arm in arm in the 'War on Terror'. What was even funnier was that both of them were standing side by side within the big tent erected by Anthony Blair, a man both of them ought privately to suspect of being a disreputable clown. I shall have to make rather a lot of use of Mr Cohen in this brief chapter, because I think it wrong to say more than a few words about a similar political journey by my brother Christopher. We have had quite enough trouble about that and I do not want to start it again. But I am quite happy to annoy Mr Cohen, and those former conservatives who have welcomed him to what they think is their side. Actually Mr Cohen has not really come any distance at all. He may well have prevented himself from undergoing a real change of mind, by having a superficial one and being praised too much for it. But the former conservatives who march alongside him in the 'War against Terror', and who supported Mr Blair and his Iraq adventure, have abandoned almost everything they ever believed in.

Mr Cohen apparently accepts the official version of the Iraq war – that it was fought in the cause of Iraqi freedom and democracy. This belief, insofar as it matters, is wholly contradicted by the facts. Mr Blair invented his passion for Iraqi liberty after other pretexts had failed. On 25 February 2003 he said:

> I do not want war. I do not believe anyone in this House wants war. But disarmament peacefully can only happen with Saddam's active cooperation. I detest his regime, but even now he can save it by complying with the United Nations demands ... the path to peace is clear.

In the same way, in the Kosovo conflict which prepared the way for the Iraq war, he developed a retrospective passion for the removal of Slobodan Milošević from power in Serbia. During the early stages of the Kosovo war, on 20 April 1999, he had unintentionally called on Mr Milošević to 'step down', during a news conference with Javier Solana of NATO, when he had meant to say 'step back'. Great efforts were devoted by NATO's official spokesman to correcting this verbal bungle.

'There is no question of making some deal or compromise with Milošević,' Mr Blair said. 'We have set out our demands and objectives and they will be met in full because they are the minimum demands that we can, in all humanity, make.' Asked about NATO's determination in light of the fact that Milošević had shown no sign of backing down, Blair said, 'The solution is very simple, we will carry on until he does step down.' Later, the NATO spokesman Jamie Shea said that NATO did not intend to force Milošević to step down from his leadership of the Balkan country, but did say bombing would continue until he 'backed down' from his refusal to accept NATO terms for peace. 'I have always said that Milošević's future is up to the Serbian people,' Shea added, in case anyone was in any doubt that the British Prime Minister had gone too far.

A few days before Mr Blair had given Saddam his 'last chance', on 15 February there was a large and mainly Left-wing demonstration against the planned war on Iraq. (*Declaration of interest*: though opposed to the war, I did not attend this demonstration because I disagreed with the protest's organisers about many important issues – notably the Israel–Palestine question – and thought most of them would have opposed a just war as readily as they opposed this unjust one. In any case I was lucky enough to be able to express my dissent through a newspaper column.) In a chapter headed 'The Disgrace of the Anti-War Movement', Nick Cohen pronounced 'On 15 February 2003, about a million liberal-minded people marched through London to oppose the overthrow of a fascist regime.'

Mr Cohen quite rightly condemned the simple-minded anti-Americanism of many of these marchers. The loathing of the USA and the rude treatment of individual Americans displayed by many on the British Left are close to racial bigotry, and they certainly played some part in this turnout. A resentful and sulky view of America and Americans is common in the British middle class, though Left-wingers and Right-wingers would be upset if this were identified as what it is – petulance at the ceding of global power status from London to Washington after the 1939–45 war. The strategic defeat of the British Empire by the USA, though one of the central events of the last century, is seldom if ever acknowledged as such. To do so would be too painful, and would upset our principal foreign alliance. Mr Cohen should know. A year before this demonstration of supposed 'fascist' supporters took place, the same Nick Cohen had written (in the *New Statesman* of 14 January 2002): 'But with no alternative to the present regime in Washington in sight, a depressingly convincing justification for anti-Americanism remains: that there is little about modern America to be for.'

But his dismissal of the marchers as 'opponents of the overthrow of a fascist regime' is the crudest trickery and misrepresentation. Let us not dwell too long on the empty use of the word 'fascist', long ago dismissed by George Orwell as meaningless (as described at length elsewhere in this book).

The slippery part is in the way the purpose of the demonstration, aimed at the British government by citizens of Britain, is falsified. It becomes instead a demonstration in defence not only of the regime of the state which is threatened with attack, but also the actual nature of that regime. This is outrageously untrue, supported neither by facts nor logic. They were protesting against their own government's actions, against their own government's involvement in a military action of which they disapproved. Their concern was their own country's use of its power. They would have protested in this way whoever and wherever the target had been because they were unconvinced by the arguments advanced in favour of the attack. The identity of the planned target was not the point, let alone the nature of the regime in the planned target. They supported (as Mr Cohen presumably supports) international law. This law, really dating from the UN's establishment in 1945, prohibits aggressive war except in circumstances which did not exist in Iraq. The issue could not, in law, have been the character of the Baghdad government.

Mr Blair (see above p. 174) would explain a few days later that he was ready to permit the continuance of Saddam's 'fascist' regime if it did as he asked. If the British government's elaborate propaganda on the subject was to be taken seriously, things were even more complicated than that. What if Iraq had been (by the curious standards of these days of 'Orange' and 'Rose' revolutions) a 'democracy', yet had been accused of stockpiling 'weapons of mass destruction'? What if it had been a 'democracy' and had been proven to possess such weapons? It is no longer true to claim that democracies do not start wars, even if you accept that Britain and the USA were legally justified in their attack on Iraq. Georgia, at the time of writing the 'democratic' ally of the USA, launched a war against (theoretically democratic) Russia in South Ossetia in August 2008 – thus also disproving the theory that countries which host McDonald's hamburger bars never go to war against each other.

Now, this trickery and misrepresentation by Mr Cohen could not have fooled a well-informed child and no doubt has not fooled the demonstrators of February 2003, who must for the most part still be congratulating themselves on being far wiser than their rulers. This same counterfeit logic could equally well be used to say of Mr Cohen's new hero, Mr Blair, that on 25 February 2003 he declared his willingness to tolerate the continued existence of a fascist regime. Mr Cohen presumably did not make this accusation because it did not suit him. Such arguments are only ever really deployed to deceive the person who is advancing them. And Mr Cohen, while not deceiving his Left-wing targets, has successfully deceived himself. Why would he have done that?

What interests me about Mr Cohen is that (as mentioned elsewhere in this book) he has also attacked the orthodoxy of the fashionable Left in a much more dangerous place – its hypocrisy over selective state education. This is a most unusual heresy and a dangerous one. Most significantly, he has also realised that crude anti-Americanism is a hangover from the Cold War. And he has probably recognised that the United States, far from being the arsenal of conservatism, is now the military wing of a utopian globalism.

But his discoveries have stopped at this point. He makes no connection between his exposure of the Left's hypocrisy about education and anything else. After all, Mr Blair, one of the principal educational hypocrites of our time, is the object of Mr Cohen's adulation.

For Mr Cohen has become, as have others on the utopian Left, an admirer of Anthony Blair's foreign policy. He has done this in spite of holding to the usual thought-free untruths about Mr Blair's government being 'Right-wing' in domestic matters, which are the received opinion of the times. This new alignment followed Mr Blair's famous Chicago speech, on 24 April 1999, in which he asserted the need to intervene for idealistic reasons in other people's countries. He overthrew, in the same few words, the hard-won wisdom of the Peace of Westphalia of 1648 and the United Nations Charter of 1945.

Such a thoughtful person as Mr Cohen, having become a critic of his own side on education and America, must have been tempted to go further into the matter, to reconsider the whole Left-wing universe. But there was no need. Because the supposed 'Right wing' had made its own equally shocking accommodation with Mr Blair's post-Chicago position, Mr Cohen could be welcomed into the new comity of freedom-lovers even if he had never uttered a word about the badness of comprehensive education. In fact, I suspect many of his admirers on the New Right do not even know that he has taken this position. More paradoxical still, Mr Cohen's strongly implied support for selection by ability places him well to the 'right' of official Tory policy on the subject, now that the Tory Party has publicly declared that it will open no more grammar schools, except perhaps in places where they already exist.

Another Left-wing journalist suddenly struck by the absurdity of his positions, Andrew Anthony appears initially to be on the high diving board, preparing to plunge into a real apostasy. Like Mr Cohen, Mr Anthony was so unsettled by his friends' anti-American responses to September 11 that he began to wonder if he was on the right side. His book *The Fallout* (Jonathan Cape, London, 2007) is much more interesting than Mr Cohen's. It is a catalogue of awakenings, on crime, Leftist excuse-making, double-think about the Soviet Union, multiculturalism, vandalism, crime, the catch-all accusation of 'racism' and the uselessness of a liberalised police force. He was almost there. Another few months and he might actually have admitted that the Left has been wrong about almost every major subject for the last fifty years, and drawn the appropriate conclusions. It is difficult not to wonder if he was aware of how close he had come to crossing the frontier that really divides radical from conservative. But, like Nick Cohen, he was saved from this course by the events of September 11, 2001. This quickly and comfortably diverted him into the war against militant Islam, where he could stand shoulder to shoulder with Charles Moore in support of

Anthony Blair and George W. Bush, and against the cloudy, permanent menace of 'Al Qaeda' and 'Islamo-Fascism'.

This is a very interesting halting place, as well as a comfortable one. For the habitual Leftist, it has the virtue of making him look as if he can change his mind, even when he has not really done so. It licenses him to be strongly anti-clerical and anti-religious, but in a way that Christian conservatives can tolerate. It enables him to resolve the absurdity of the mainstream Left's desire to appease Islam in the cause of multiculturalism. He can obtain much pleasure from attacking Islam for its attitude towards women and homosexuals, its general obscurantism and its intolerance. It allows him to pose as the defender of 'democracy' and even 'freedom' in Iraq and Afghanistan, against 'fascistic' Baathists and Taleban militants. He can be so fervent about this that he can quietly forget that the same people have been his allies in the past, in the struggle against Zionism and against British monoculture. He can also forget that the War on Terror has allies, and has used methods, which are no more democratic in reality than the Baath Party or the Taleban. This position requires its holder to regard a vote, however dubious, sectarian or foregone, as a sort of sacramental blessing on the regime which is installed by it. This has the side-effect of obliging its holder to take an uncritical view of such suspect events as the 'Orange Revolution' in Ukraine and the 'Rose Revolution' in Georgia. And, as we shall see, it involves him in the invention of a manufactured and fake 'New Cold War' against Russia.

But the chief joy of the Leftist supporter of regime change is that his new opinion permits him to be warlike, patriotic and radical at once. It allows him to recognise an essential truth about many political conservatives: that they are not after all the monsters of myth, but in most cases perfectly civilised human beings with generous instincts and a desire for a better world. In all these ways it allows him to come closer to reality. But it diverts almost all his passions into foreign policy, where he can sustain this unlikely coalition without needing to rebuild the rest of his world-view or become involved in the weary detail of taxation, marriage, immigration, welfare and crime. In these flat, unappealing fields of endeavour, unpleasant, unpopular and difficult choices face the serious reformer. No wonder professional politicians and pundits prefer not to venture into them, and are only too happy to be diverted into the simple, uplifting picturesque highlands of foreign policy and reforming the world.

One of the most striking things about both 'neo-conservatives' and their allies among the renegade Left is how uninterested they seem to be in domestic policy nowadays. The renegade's apparent conversion turns out to be yet another version of consensus. It does not bring him into real adversarial conflict with conventional wisdom. It delivers him to another portion of the 'centre ground', one where foreign policy is the only thing worth discussing, and where former conservatives and former Leftists can mingle in happy communion as long as both forget that they ever cared about the pre-2001 culture wars. They have two things in common. They are ferociously hostile to Islamism and they are – at the very least – uninterested in conservative social, cultural or moral policies. They are also remarkably uninterested in the real threat to British national independence and our 'way of life' posed by the European Union, an issue which has mysteriously died among conventional conservatives since 2001, and which the Left quietly forgot in the late 1980s.

For the former conservative, the 'War on Terror' is a pleasing and comfortable replacement for the Cold War. It provides a sinister and wicked enemy who is everywhere in the world. The enemy has agents in our own population, and fellow-travellers too gullible to realise the wickedness of the cause they aid. There is no likely – let alone immediate – prospect of ultimate victory. The nation must be permanently at war and in a sort of state of emergency for as far ahead as the eye can see. It binds us even more closely to the United States in a sentimental brotherhood, delaying still further the unpleasant recognition that the USA has been Britain's principal rival for the past century, and has comprehensively overcome us. It provides the feeling of noble action, among two groups which have largely given up hope of achieving their domestic goals.

How has this happened?

Charles Moore, who seemed to be thoroughly conservative when I first met him in the 1980s, loathed Mr Blair and everything he stood for, for many years. He was particularly scathing about Mr Blair towards the end of his first government, when he denounced the 'forces of conservatism'. These were forces Mr Moore loved, ancient institutions, the armed forces, tradition and religion. They were the opposite of the colour-TV, Rolling Stones, rock-and-roll world which Mr Blair had explicitly endorsed. Even within the Labour Party, Mr Blair scorned his movement's traditional parts, the majestic red and gold Trade Union banners, the temperance and Methodist legacy, the dusty committee rooms, the dedicated ward meetings, the talk of brothers and sisters – and of course the sentimental singing of 'The Red Flag' not because anyone believed in it but because it had always been sung.

Mr Blair was also opposed vigorously – in his early, less warlike years – by less traditional Conservatives such as Michael Gove. Mr Gove did not share Charles Moore's enthusiasm for Roman Catholicism, hunting and rectories. But he regarded himself as being separated from Mr Blair by many potent issues, economic and political. He was also not in those days noticeably religious, while Mr Blair was. But, like Mr Blair, he was on the radical side of the debates about homosexual partnerships and similar measures. This was not enough for him to identify himself as a Blairite, as he would later. (By a charming paradox, as Mr Gove has become less conservative he appears to have become more religious, to the extent that, as noted in Chapter 12, he has sent his eldest child to a Church of England primary school and his wife works diligently for the parish magazine of the relevant church.)

But the 'War on Terror' provided both Mr Moore and Mr Gove with a rope-bridge across the chasm which had

until then separated them from the then Prime Minister. Mr
Moore, having decided to support Mr Blair in the 'War on
Terror', has since become a militant defender of the 'Centre
Left' Conservative Party of David Cameron, the self-proclaimed
'heir to Blair'. From my recollection of his table talk when we
lunched ministers together in the 1980s, and of the *Spectator*
which he edited at the time, the Cameron Tory Party contains
many features which Mr Moore would have despised in the
days of Margaret Thatcher and John Major, and come to that
in the early days of Anthony Blair. Mr Gove has gone even
further than Mr Moore. In *The Times* of 25 February 2003, he
wrote an astonishing article about how he had all but fallen in
love with Mr Blair. It is worth quoting at length. It ran:

> You could call it the Elizabeth Bennett moment. It's what
> Isolde felt when she fell into Tristan's arms. It's the point you
> reach when you give up fighting your feelings, abandon the
> antipathy bred into your bones, and admit that you were
> wrong about the man. By God, it's still hard to write this,
> but I'm afraid I've got to be honest. Tony Blair is proving an
> outstanding Prime Minister at the moment.
>
> This news is, of course, the last thing the Prime Minister
> needs. Mr Blair faces a difficult enough task in the
> Commons today trying to rally the Labour Party behind his
> Iraq policy without Tory Boys in the pay of global press
> magnates slavering all over him.
>
> And many, but far from all, of my fellow rightwingers will
> wonder what on earth I'm doing licking Mr Blair's boots
> when Labour are, at last, dipping in the polls.
>
> Shouldn't any Conservative-inclined commentator be
> turning up the heat on the Prime Minister now, at last,
> when he's vulnerable? Don't the Tories have enough internal
> problems without those writers who're supposed to be
> sympathetic to their cause bigging up Blair?
>
> They're all good points if you're a tribalist. But I'm a
> journalist. In so far as I'm sympathetic to Tory politicians,
> and their arguments, it's because as a right-wing polemicist

I find them persuasive. And as a right-wing polemicist, all I can say looking at Mr Blair now is, what's not to like?

Central to any current assessment of Mr Blair has to be the manner in which he is handling the Iraq crisis. But before considering just how impressive his stance is, and how petty his detractors, it's worth noting that Mr Blair's entitlement to conservative respect doesn't rest on his foreign policy alone.

He then praises, rather extravagantly, several domestic policies in which Mr Blair appeared to be following more or less Thatcherite paths:

The Prime Minister has been right, and brave, to introduce market pressures into higher education by pushing through university top-up fees in the teeth of opposition from his egalitarian Chancellor. He's been correct in conceding, to the annoyance of his wife I'm sure, that the European Convention on Human Rights gets in the way of a sane asylum policy. In dealing with the firefighters, and their absurdly selfish strike, he's been satisfactorily resolute.

There are certainly idiocies aplenty across the range of this Government's domestic policy, indeed that's hardly surprising given ministers like Tessa Jowell and John Prescott in the Cabinet. The problem with putting muppets into office is that there's no one left to pull the strings when your hands are full.

While we're on the subject of pulling strings, the Government will also struggle to improve public services while it continues to rely on centralised funding, management and provision. But even here, Mr Blair and some of his smarter ministers, such as Alan Milburn, the Health Secretary, seem to be acknowledging the limitations of their tax, spend, command and control strategy.

In truth, these supposedly conservative actions look fairly thin five years later. But they also provide the first embryonic version of what was to become Cameron conservatism – an explicit identification with Mr Blair and an acceptance of the dubious claim that he was engaged in some sort of conflict with 'Brownites' who persisted in defending high public spending and statism against Mr Blair's supposed market instincts. The fact that the Labour government hugely expanded tax, government spending and state control during Mr Blair's period in office does not seem to in any way undermine or weaken this strange belief.

As so often on the centre ground, it is the former conservatives who have to concede, abandon or quietly forget old positions, and to heap praise upon the gimmicks of the Left. They have to do this, or they will not be allowed to stand on the 'centre ground'. The Left, by contrast, are not required to make any serious changes to their beliefs, only to the way in which they express them. The egalitarian principle is still the beating heart of Labour thinking. No wonder Mr Gove returned so swiftly to the safety zone area of foreign affairs, where militant atheist Leftist 'pro-democracy' fantasists could stand hand in hand with equally idealist churchgoing neo-conservative schemers, both convinced they had it in their power to begin the world over again.

Mr Gove was clearly more comfortable when he steered his pro-Blair article into overseas matters:

> It is not, however, on the domestic agenda that Mr Blair is facing his biggest challenge at the moment. It is over Iraq that he is in greatest difficulty politically. All because, as a Labour Prime Minister, he's behaving like a true Thatcherite.
>
> Indeed, he's braver in some respects than Maggie was. The Falklands war took courage. But Thatcher had most of the country, and her party, behind her. In dealing with the Iraq crisis, Mr Blair has neither.
>
> The Thatcherite approach to foreign policy isn't to every Tory taste. The belief that dictators should be confronted, not coddled, America is there to be supported, not patronised, and the national interest includes maintaining our

honour not just calculating narrow advantage, is depre-
cated by some Conservatives.

They include a lot of clever people, from Matthew Parris
to Chris Patten.

But if ever I'm tempted to think these Tories may perhaps
have a point, I just look at who's enraged by the
Thatcherite stance that Mr Blair has adopted towards
Iraq. Any policy that unites George Galloway, Vanessa
Redgrave, Jacques Chirac, the Bishop of Oxford, George
Michael and Piers Morgan in condemnation has to have
something going for it. And Mr Blair's policy has more
than just the right critics. It has the merit of genuine moral
force.

As the Prime Minister has pointed out, all those opposed
to him have no solution to the problem of proliferating
weapons of mass destruction, they offer no hope to the
people of Iraq, they have no understanding of how much
every tyrant and terrorist across the globe would rejoice if
the West were to back down in the face of President
Saddam Hussein's brinksmanship.

I would insert here that people such as Michael Gove (and
people such as Nick Cohen) seldom if ever engaged with
conservative critics of the Iraq war, or even admitted their
existence. Both dismissed the anti-war (or in Nick Cohen's
case 'pro-fascist') movement as a rabble of Trotskyists,
woolly Bishops, Bennites or Islamists. They ignored those
who argued against the war on the basis of national sovereignty and of a proper scepticism about propaganda. Even
to have recognised that we existed would have been
damaging to their case.

Let us return for a moment to the religious part of this
paradox. Like Michael Gove, Charles Moore and Andrew
Anthony, Nick Cohen is an astute and experienced journalist.
He must know that many of the beliefs of the mainstream Left
are false, many of the consequences of Left-wing utopianism
unintended and unpleasant. He is by no means a fool, but he

is committed, probably above all else, to the idea that he rules himself. He is a 'secular humanist'.

Now, the Left's wholly ridiculous affair with Islam has provided the more acute radicals with a welcome way out of a problem. By denouncing Islamism, and Islam, they dodge what might otherwise be a nasty choice between experiencing a full-scale epiphany or of drowning their doubts, like so many defenceless kittens. Under the neo-conservative dispensation, they can continue to condemn religious faith, as fiercely and contemptuously as possible. Yet at the same time they can break wholly and forever with many of the most alarming idiocies of the twenty-first-century Left, including anti-Americanism and apologising for terrorist acts.

The formula has some problems. It does not fully solve the semi-apostate's difficulty with the State of Israel, which has become a pariah country in the minds of almost all radicals. But it serves to conceal it.

The quarrel about Israel (rather like the other forgotten argument about the European Union) has suffered a remarkable eclipse since 2001. This is very odd. The confrontation between the USA and Islam in the Middle East is in reality almost entirely the result of American support for Israel.

But it is instead attributed to an alleged 'hatred of our way of life' supposedly felt by all Muslims. The anti-Israel elements of September 11 are forgotten, or denied any significance. These facts are relevant. The Arab TV station Al Jazeera, in September 2002, aired a pre-suicide video by Abdul-Aziz al-Omari, one of the hijacker-murderers of 11 September 2001. Al-Omari is believed by the FBI to be responsible for hijacking the American Airlines plane which was flown into the north tower of the World Trade Center. Al-Omari, a Saudi Arabian national, was shown in the film wearing a chequered 'keffiyeh' headscarf, often adopted by supporters of the Palestinian Arab cause (reported by AFP 9 September 2002). Al-Omari stated in his film that the September 11 attacks were to be 'a message to all infidels and to America to leave the Arabian peninsula and stop supporting the cowardly Jews in Palestine'. What better evidence of the hijackers' true mind could we ask for than the words of one of them, spoken shortly before he committed his crime?

This is not all. The September 11 attack was generally understood in the Middle East to be connected with the Israel–Palestine issue. A report by the *Washington Post's* Lee Hockstader, also carried by several other major US dailies, recorded on 16 September 2001 that the Palestinian Authority had been trying to suppress film taken of Palestinian Arabs in East Jerusalem celebrating the outrage. 'Palestinian officials have told local representatives of foreign news agencies and television stations on several occasions that their employees' safety could be jeopardized if videotapes showing Palestinians celebrating the attacks were aired. Broadcast news organizations operating in the Palestinian-ruled portions of the West Bank and Gaza Strip have complied.'

On 17 September 2001 the *Milwaukee Journal Sentinel* reported:

> The Palestinian Authority on Sunday returned a videotape it had confiscated two days earlier from The Associated Press, but removed were parts of a protest rally led by the militant Islamic group Hamas. About 1,500 Palestinians, many supporters of Hamas, marched in a Gaza Strip refugee camp on Friday, burning Israeli flags and carrying a poster of Osama bin Laden, named by the U.S. government as the leading suspect in the terror attacks in the United States.
>
> After the rally, plainclothes Palestinian police questioned several journalists and confiscated videotape and film from at least four news organizations. AP news wires reported on the demonstration, and the poster of bin Laden that was raised during the rally. The Palestinian Authority has sought to prevent coverage of demonstrations in support of the attacks on the World Trade Center in New York and the Pentagon in Washington.

A similar report in the *Seattle Times* on the same day noted:

> Yasser Arafat's Palestinian Authority is trying to suppress broadcast images and photos of Palestinians glorifying the terrorist attacks on the United States and hailing the suspected mastermind, Osama bin Laden.
>
> The suppression of the images is part of a campaign by Arafat and his lieutenants to avoid being perceived in the West as part of the international terrorist scourge. Having sided with Iraq during the Persian Gulf War, the Palestinians are eager to avoid a similar political blunder, analysts say.
>
> Palestinian officials acknowledge suppressing the images, arguing they distorted public opinion and would be used by Israel to mount a smear campaign against Arafat and his government.
>
> 'These measures were not against the freedom of the press but in order to ensure our national security and our national interest,' said Yasser Abed Rabbo, the Palestinian information minister. 'We will not permit a few kids here or there to smear the real face of the Palestinians. This is a real insult to our people and our nation.'
>
> Meanwhile, Arafat was filmed donating blood for victims in Washington and New York, and he seemed suddenly more receptive to negotiations with the Israelis. Palestinian schoolchildren were made to stand in silence to commemorate the victims, Palestinian officials and journalists signed a petition of sympathy, and the Palestinian Legislative Council met in a special session to express its grief.
>
> Palestinians also held a candlelight vigil outside the U.S. Consulate in East Jerusalem.

But there was more:

> Still, many Palestinians deeply resent the United States for supporting Israel and supplying weapons that have been

used against them in the past year's Middle East violence. On several occasions since Tuesday, those sentiments have burst into public view.

Hours after the attacks, Associated Press Television videotaped a small group of Palestinians, some of them children, rejoicing in East Jerusalem. That footage infuriated Americans and alarmed Palestinian officials, who moved swiftly to block the release of similar images.

Elisabetta Burba, an Italian writing in the Wall Street Journal a few days after the Manhattan massacre, reported a similar understanding of the nature and message of the September 11 attack, from Beirut.

Once back at the house where we were staying, we started scanning the international channels. Soon came reports of Palestinians celebrating. The BBC reporter in Jerusalem said it was only a tiny minority. Astonished, we asked some moderate Arabs if that was the case. 'Nonsense,' said one, speaking for many. 'Ninety percent of the Arab world believes that Americans got what they deserved.'

'An exaggeration?' she asked. Then she answered her own question:

Rather an understatement. A couple of days later, we headed north to Tripoli, near the Syrian border. On the way, we read that Palestinian leader Yasser Arafat, who donated blood in front of the cameras, was rejecting any suggestion that his people were rejoicing over the terrorist attack. 'It was less than 10 children in Jerusalem,' he said.

In the bustling souk of Tripoli we started looking for the Great Mosque, a 1294 building with a distinctive Lombard-style tower ... Once at the mosque I donned a black chador, but our Lonely Planet guide attracted the attention of a hard-looking bearded guy all the same.

'Are you Americans?' he asked in a menacing tone. Our quick denial made him relax. He gave us the green light to go in. But very soon afterward we were again approached, by a fat young man. He turned out to be one of the 350,000 Palestinians who live in Lebanon, unwelcome by most of the population and subject to severe hardships ... he soon moved on to politics and the 'events.'

'My people have been crushed under the heel of American imperialism, which took away our land, massacred our beloved and denied our right to life. But have you seen what happened in New York City? God Almighty has drawn his sword against our enemies. God is great – *Allah u Akbar*,' he said.

On 13 September 2001, Matthew Kalman reported in *USA Today*:

Arab League spokeswoman Hanan Ashrawi hastily organized a candlelight vigil at the U.S. Consulate in East Jerusalem nearly 24 hours after hundreds of Israelis flocked to the U.S. Embassy in Tel Aviv in a spontaneous outpouring of grief.

Palestinian Cabinet Secretary Ahmed Abdel Rahman used tougher measures to avoid an international backlash in response to apparent Palestinian jubilation. Abdel Rahman called international news agencies and said the safety of their staff could not be guaranteed unless they withdrew the embarrassing footage of Palestinian police firing joyfully in the air. Such threats appeared to succeed in suppressing immediate release of video showing large street celebrations in Ramallah, Bethlehem and other West Bank towns.

In slightly different circumstances, this grisly blackmail, combined with ghoulish rejoicing over bloodshed, would have become a major theme in news reports. Because it did not fit with the conventional wisdom, that September 11 was an 'Al Qaeda' attack connected with Afghanistan and an 'attack on our way of life', it featured more strongly in provincial newspapers than it did in major metropolitan ones – even though it was written by a member of the *Washington Post* staff. Something similar would be true a year later when Al-Omari's video was shown. I recall it being briefly aired, but being little commented on and not repeated, unlike so much other footage dealing with that event. Once again, it did not fit the narrative demanded by conventional wisdom.

In the light of these contemporary reports – which may have gone largely unnoticed because most eyes were still turned towards New York – and in the light of the actual statement made by one of the murderers – it is remarkable that so many supporters of the 'War on Terror' (both pre-existing neo-conservatives and Left-wing opponents of 'Islamo-Fascism') object when it is suggested that the September 11 attacks are part of the Arab–Israel conflict. Yet it is possible to see why it would suit both groups. The neo-conservatives, being committed supporters of Zionism, might find it unsettling to admit that the USA's support for Israel came at such a high price. They might also be ashamed of Washington's obvious desire to truckle to Islamic terror in the weeks after the attack (see below).

The Left-wing converts to the use of American power against Muslims would not want to think that this placed them, even directly, among the supporters of the Zionist state. Hence the exaggerated importance, to both groups, of the nebulous grouping termed 'Al Qaeda' and the under-playing of the Israeli issue.

It is also necessary to note that the September 11 atrocities took place very shortly after an extraordinary verbal and moral conflict between the Muslim world and Israel (and the USA) at the United Nations world conference 'against racism, racial discrimination, xenophobia and related intolerance' at Durban from 31 August to 7 September 2001. The US and Israeli delegations walked out on 3 September, in protest at what they regarded as blatant uncontrolled hostility towards Israel.

Colin Powell, then US Secretary of State, said

> I know that you do not combat racism by conferences that produce declarations containing hateful language, some of which is a throwback to the days of 'Zionism equals racism'; or supports the idea that we have made too much of the Holocaust; or suggests that apartheid exists in Israel; or that singles out only one country in the world, Israel, for censure and abuse.

Israel's then Foreign Minister, Shimon Peres called the South African conference an 'unbelievable attempt to smear Israel'. 'An important convention that's supposed to defend human rights became a source of hatred,' Peres said. 'We knew from the start we didn't stand a chance of convincing the leagues of hatred but we had some respect for other countries.'

It is in any case perfectly obvious to anyone with any experience of travelling in the Middle East, or of conversations with politically aware Arabs, that the issue of Israel is the principal and often the only subject which they wish to discuss with Westerners, and the one over which there is most complete agreement among Arabs of all nations and classes, and one of the very few points on which Arab Sunnis and Iranian Shias are in agreement. (I do not say this because I share this view. I am a Zionist and supporter of Israel, who has also reported from several Arab countries and from Iran, and believes the USA is right to support Israel's existence.)

The response of the USA to the September 11 attacks was also an implicit recognition that the problem, and the cause of the attack, was US policy on Israel. Among the US government's first clear post-attack actions (on 25 September) was the payment of many millions of dollars in back dues to the very UN it had so recently condemned for prejudice against Israel (by handing over this cash, it threw away a powerful weapon in its constant and correct pursuit of necessary UN reform). The

US troops in Saudi Arabia were withdrawn, as Ol-Omari had demanded. The decision was formally announced in April 2003, probably the earliest moment possible without the connection being obvious. Before that there were several attempts to negotiate with the presumed political wing of the movement which had attacked Manhattan. There were repeated missions to Yasser Arafat, first by General Anthony Zinni in November and December 2001 and March 2002, and then by Colin Powell himself in April 2002. All these visits were in fact destabilised by Palestinian violence, including suicide attacks on Israelis – signs either that Yasser Arafat did not control his militants or that he wished to increase the pressure on Washington by the crudest means.

Perhaps the single most significant change was President George W. Bush's declaration of support for a Palestinian state, made on 10 October 2001. This, in any other circumstances, would have been a major event and a subject of great controversy. When in May 1998 Hillary Clinton had made a similar statement it was swiftly disavowed by the White House. Mrs Clinton is and was a Leftish Democrat. Mr Bush is supposedly a conservative Republican. What except September 11 can have made Mr Bush more radical than Mrs Clinton?

The Machiavellian Israeli Prime Minister, Ariel Sharon, managed to head off these initiatives by appropriating the same 'War on Terror' rhetoric being used by the White House. He cunningly persuaded American public opinion that Israel shared America's suffering and was an equal ally. The combination of Arafat's ineptitude and Sharon's devious cynicism destroyed what would otherwise have almost certainly been yet another major American effort to force Israel into large territorial and diplomatic concessions, the first since the failure of the Clinton Camp David and Taba plans and the resulting collapse of the Israeli peace coalition.

No doubt Nick Cohen, and Left-liberal secularists like him, would be supporters of such a 'peace process' and of pressure upon Israel to retreat into a still smaller space. That is to say, in this case, they would be glad to see concessions to the 'Islamo-Fascists' and 'obscurantists' whom they claim utterly to despise. But fortunately for the consistency of their arguments, this process is currently completely halted. Oddly enough, the procedure known as 'land for peace' in which Israel gives up sizeable pieces of real property, important to its defence, in return for unenforceable paper promises, is the closest modern Western diplomacy actually comes to the Anglo-French treatment of Czechoslovakia in 1938. Fortunately, Neville Chamberlain never had the wit to use the expression 'land for peace', so – while the parallel is a cliché in Israel, it is little noticed in Europe or the USA.

No wonder the neo-conservatives, and their Left-wing allies, prefer to concentrate on the supposedly simpler issues of the 'Al Qaeda' threat and of Iraqi 'Weapons of Mass Destruction'. If they fell to arguing about Israel, their coalition would be over in minutes. Best avoid the subject altogether, and pretend it has nothing to do with the matter. Claims that 'Muslims hate our way of life' allow these two utterly different groups to feel an affinity against a common enemy. Actually, a proper conservative Christian (though not a neo-conservative one) also 'hates our way of life', at least those parts of it which are based upon adultery, fornication, the overthrow of parental authority, licentiousness, self-stupefaction and debt. But the neo-conservatives are deeply uninterested in this sort of conservatism, and often actively hostile to it. They are far more interested in the free market and also in the 'free movement of labour'. The latter, which involves open borders, is in fact the main engine of Islamisation in Europe (though not yet in the USA, where mass immigration is mainly Hispanic). Neo-conservatism actually has much more in common with Marxist utopi-anism than it does with sceptical, particular conservatism. This is why Nick Cohen, and people like him, find it so easy to get on with neo-conservatives.

In these two matching but opposite reactions, we see that the alliance between these two groups is essentially false and unsustainable. Neo-conservatives do not hate religion as such (though they have a hard spot for Islam). The Nick Cohen group still think Israel is a colonialist interloper, and would overlook the 'Islamo-Fascist' nature of the Palestinian cause if they possibly could. This is not a real road to Damascus, just a comfortable hotel on the way there, where both sides have chosen to stay in convivial if shallow companionship, rather than reaching the ultimate destinations of their thoughts.

The sad and unsatisfactory side of this is that Left-wing dogmatists can appear to change their minds, and be given credit (or be enjoyably attacked by their former comrades) for having done so, without undergoing any true revolution. These false epiphanies obscure the fact that the Left, having been proved wrong by events for decades, still declines to admit that it has ever been wrong. They also allow political conservatism to soothe its tribal base by appearing strong and militant overseas, while failing to be anything of the kind at home.

Conclusion:
The Broken Compass

When Britain dies, which seems likely to happen quite soon, it will be difficult for the chief mourners to decide exactly what to say at the funeral, or what to inscribe on the national tombstone. Not many are now alive who will remember what the deceased was like when he still had his health and strength. Those who knew him in his final declining years, his memory failing, his muscles withered, his estates sold off, chasing after get-rich-quick schemes and silly fashions, found it hard to imagine why he had been both so much beloved and so much hated in his prime.

But at the reading of the will, one part of the legacy will be valued above all others. This will be the extraordinary achievement of orderly freedom, under a law mainly made by those who obeyed it. When the dusty old box is opened, in which this lovely, delicate and long unused mechanism is contained, it will be found that one of its most important components is the adversarial system, in which True Left and True Right, neatly counterbalanced, fight forever against each other. But it can no longer be set in motion, for the political compass once used to calibrate these things has somehow been broken and its needle swings vaguely around, indicating nothing in particular. What a loss this is.

By a series of happy accidents our Parliament was based upon the idea that two sides needed to argue their case before any important matter was decided.

Few of us are wise enough to recognise the truth the first time we see it. The cleverest of us are often wrong. Argument with an opponent is the best form of education known to man. And in debates about the ordering of society two rival ideas of goodness, loved by their adherents as much as they are loathed by their opponents, have contended for centuries. One is based on a belief in Original Sin, the other on a belief in the perfectibility of man. Out of this battle have come many civilised and unsatisfactory compromises – which for all their grubbiness have been hugely preferable to the bloody, world-reforming zeal unleashed on less happy lands. It is not an accident that a country with a Gold State Coach, Erskine May, a Lord Chancellor and a Black Rod is also a country without a secret police force or torture chambers, where the police cannot stop you and demand your papers. Or so it was.

I do not know whether this contest had its roots in the ancient hostility between Norman and Saxon, or in the English Civil War, or in the British class system. It does not much matter. What is certain is that in the last thirty years it has almost completely ceased. Parliamentary politics have come to revolve almost entirely round personality and petty scandal. The formerly sedate House of Lords has become the more interesting chamber, partly because the Commons has grown so dull, partly because the House of Peers, in its role as eventide home for politicians, contains so many survivors of a more adversarial era.

If the end of these mental and verbal hostilities could be shown to be a good thing, then this would not matter. But it seems clear to me that our country is worse governed than it used to be, and also more governed. Bad decisions are constantly made, and increasingly hard to escape in a nation where private life is rapidly retreating into remote corners. Worst of all, a powerful political class are united on several controversial issues – from national independence to the nature of criminal justice – where their views are quite different from much of the population. Political parties have become devices for representing the views of the establishment to the people, rather than the other way round. As a result, they often embrace policies and positions which are absurd or contradictory.

The end of the Cold War, which made many of the old political positions meaningless overnight, is involved. Why has this happened? The decay of the old establishment, which accepted the adversarial arrangement has something to do with it. And that – as discussed in my *Abolition of Britain* – has many causes going back at least to 1914. Fabian social democracy has been remarkably successful in spreading its ideas into all three major political parties, so shrinking the amount of disagreement and debate. But another process, also examined in that book, has spread through the university-educated part of the population. The ideology of the 1960s, a semi-conscious mixture of Karl Marx, Leon Trotsky, Herbert Marcuse, Margaret Mead, Alfred Kinsey, Sigmund Freud, Wilhelm Reich, Antonio Gramsci, R.D. Laing, Timothy Leary, Ken Kesey, Marie Stopes, Monty Python, John Lennon and Mick Jagger, has become near-universal.

It is in many ways more of a style or an attitude than a coherent belief system. Its engine is the happy, optimistic selfishness, and the general reaction against a drab and narrow past, encouraged by post-war upbringings. It is ideally suited to the needs of the trades and professions where it is almost universal, especially television and the academy. It is so relaxed in its demeanour, charming, tieless and vague that its furious, hissing intolerance of dissent always comes as a shock. Yet it is a fact. Its members think that *they* are the dissenters and the revolutionaries, since this is how they flattered themselves, and were flattered by their parents and teachers in their days of lazing on college lawns. They also believe that their victory was total. Disagreement, especially from one of their own generation, enrages them. In their eyes, I am a generational traitor.

Yet the confidence is not justified. Many of the arguments they regard as closed demand to be reopened. Millions of children – and adults – suffer from the dissolution of marriage. The poor are cheated by atrocious schools, and victimised by unrestrained criminals. The abandonment of manners and self-restraint has made life uglier and more dangerous. Women are more chained to their workplaces than they ever were to the kitchen sink, and they fear the onset of old age more than at any time in history. Government is increasingly unable to perform simple tasks. Idealist wars end just like the old cynical wars, with acres of graves and legions of cripples hobbling through the remainder of their lives, vast numbers of human beings impoverished and displaced, and nothing good achieved. Even the educated know less than they used to. Mass immigration has radically changed the lives of many who were never asked what they thought about this. The loss of national independence has eviscerated politics. The loss of the particular and the known makes huge numbers feel homeless and alone. Yet the 'Centre Left' veers away from all these matters, unwilling to address the difficult questions they raise, and inclined to dismiss those who do raise them as bigots.

Not surprisingly, this means that professional politicians, even where they recognise that these problems exist, fear to speak about them. It also means that real bigots are left free to exploit these discontents, with growing success. And so, driven out of Parliament, where it was a benevolent thing, the adversarial system finds its way back on to the streets where I fear it will not be so benevolent.

Postscript

While I was completing this book, two powerful waves were washing across the British political landscape. I believe that both of these will eventually recede, and that the map I have tried to provide here will still be useful. But as I write this, towards the end of January 2009, I feel it would be wrong to ignore several developments.

The first of these is the banking collapse, whose end is still unknown and which may well be the beginning of a long and deep recession in which Britain's social and cultural decline will become more marked and less easy to avoid.

The second is the rally to the flag within 'New Labour', especially by Lord Mandelson, main architect and sustainer of the original Blair project.

The banking collapse has its origins in the creation and exploitation of dangerously easy credit by both banks and the state, and of the abuse of such credit by individuals. Most cautious and experienced people of all classes were rightly suspicious of this process, but unable to influence it by their actions or votes. Many were perturbed by the disappearance of the old, visible manufacturing economy, and the new reliance upon intangibles. Again, they were unable to influence this development and frequently assured by supposed experts that there was nothing to fear. Properly conservative politicians, bankers and individuals would never have engaged in such practices, and the mess we now face has much to do with the general abandonment of the sterner virtues in private and public life, as well as the crowd-pleasing politics which populist democracy tends to create.

But since no important parliamentary force now stands for those virtues, none has been able to take much advantage of the catastrophe. New Labour was plainly at least complicit and at worst directly responsible. The Tory Party, through its swooning embrace of the free market as the answer to all questions, cannot really claim to have either seen the problem coming or to have warned against it. At the time of writing, neither front bench appears to have the faintest idea what to do about it. It is hard to tell, just now, whether we are in the deceptively calm water before the lip of Niagara, or if we must just accept several years of unpleasant and unhappy events as we recover.

Perhaps as a result of this, the crisis has – so far – changed the political balance less than it might have done. The opinion poll gap between New Labour and the Tories was unrealistically, almost hysterically wide before the slide began. It then narrowed sharply as the bad news arrived. This was an understandable desire to keep a hold of nurse, for fear of finding something worse. But the obvious culpability of Gordon Brown himself, combined with the growing feeling that he does not actually understand what is going on, has caused his popularity to shrivel quite swiftly. The Tory lead has grown, but is not as absurdly huge as it was. This is partly because of the embarrassing affair of George Osborne, the Shadow Chancellor, and the Russian Oligarch's Yacht, in which Mr Osborne managed to look shifty and inexperienced. Mr Osborne, rather obscure and unadmired by almost anyone outside his immediate circle, was suddenly famous for the wrong reasons.

The voters appeared to be saying, at the start of 2009, that they were sick to death of Mr Brown, but not by any means in love with the Conservative Party. At a General Election, should there be one soon, this could present Her Majesty with an interesting and awkward choice of possible Prime Ministers. No party can be sure of gaining an absolute majority, the position of the Liberal Democrats is unclear, and the party with the greatest number of votes might well not be the party with the greatest number of seats, which raises questions of which is more legitimate. Any government resulting from such an election would be forced to rely in some way on the Liberal Democrats and so be even more bound by the 'Centre Left' consensus than if it had a majority of its own. It might also be engulfed or crushed in another sudden collapse of part of the economy, an event nobody can now rule out.

There is another unpleasant possibility. The British National Party (BNP), a disreputable but increasingly slick organisation with a plausible leader and a carefully assembled populist manifesto, might now make serious gains at the edges of British politics. These would not be enough to make it important in its own right. But they might provide the foundations for much more significant growth of this kind of politics in the future. I find this prospect frightening. One of the most potent arguments for the creation of a genuinely conservative parliamentary party, led by civilised and thoughtful men and women, is that without such a party the BNP might become an important force, something that has not happened in British politics before, but which would be highly dangerous in a period of growing unemployment, falling living standards and failing expectations in parts of the country which have until now been immune to these things.

The rallying of the Labour clan is, at first sight, hard to reconcile with the theme of this book. I have suggested that many supporters of Mr Blair would be happy to see Gordon Brown defeated at the coming election, and relaxed about leaving their project in the hands of David Cameron. I have also suggested that defections from New Labour to the Tories might take place. Given the extraordinary speed with which the fortunes of the parties change, in this era of feverish opinion, these things may yet happen – especially if Gordon Brown is overthrown by economic catastrophe.

But in January 2009, such defections seemed unlikely. Had the economic crisis not arrived to save Mr Brown from near-oblivion, they would have taken place. Early in 2008, it appeared for a while that Mr Cameron was likely to win a two-Parliament premiership. Mr Brown was counted so hopeless and unattractive that it was thought nothing could save his party. I have to admit that, precisely because I did not wish this to happen, I was one of those who came to believe that this was true after the Crewe and Nantwich by-election provided the Tories with their first significant by-election gain, and even more so after Labour's vote collapsed in Glasgow East. New Labour appeared to be suffering from a sort of political flesh-eating disease. The Tories might not be able to win the next election, but they would become the government because Labour were bound to lose it.

During the party conference season of autumn 2008, I realised that this was no longer so. Mr Brown took advantage of the economic despond to destroy his main challenger, David Miliband. In doing so he showed himself a harder and more impressive politician than most had believed. The verbal rapier which he drove through Mr Miliband's chest with the words 'This is no time for a novice' carried on to pierce Mr Cameron's ribcage too. The effect on the polls, noted above, was enough to persuade career politicians that this was also no time to leap overboard. What if, as in Joseph Conrad's *Lord Jim*, they took to the boats only to find that the stricken vessel had actually survived, making them look like panicking fools?

If they could not take to the boats, then it made sense for them to man the pumps, even though they continued to mistrust and dislike the captain. If they could come safe to harbour, they could get rid of him later. If the ship sank, it would not be their fault, but his, so they would be better placed in the recrimination that followed. The prospect – however faint – of continuing to have their hands on the levers of patronage and power, which they had thought lost for years to come, must also have moved them.

I do not believe that their attitudes have changed. I do not believe that they view Mr Cameron as a threat to their political aims. But they do view him as a threat – which might conceivably still be defeated – to their positions of influence and grandeur. So for the moment, they think it wise to try to save Mr Brown, if only in order to destroy him later. They support him, but only as the rope supports the hanged man.

Index